ADULT COLORING BOOKS

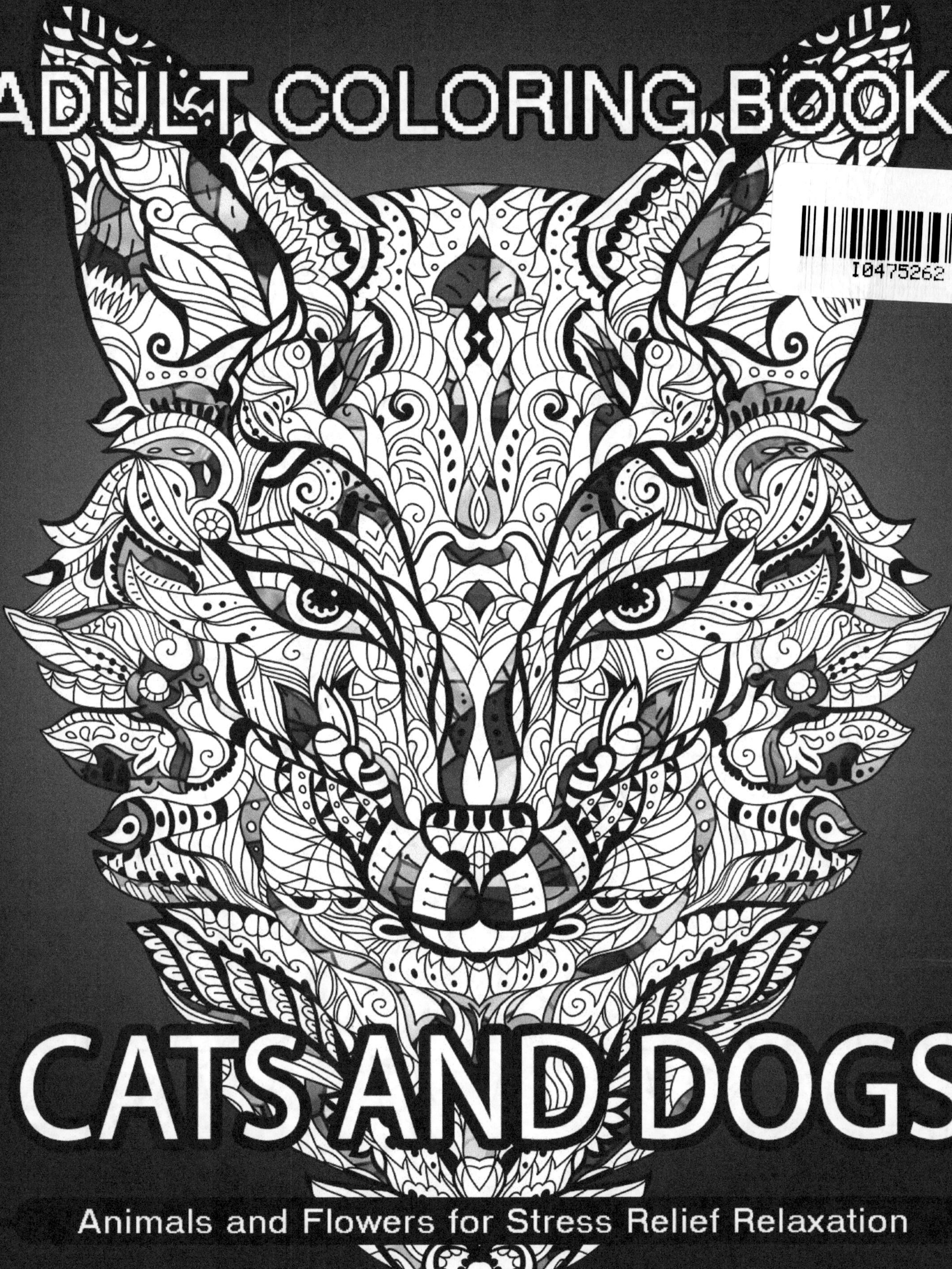

CATS AND DOGS

Animals and Flowers for Stress Relief Relaxation

TEST YOUR COLOR

TEST YOUR COLOR

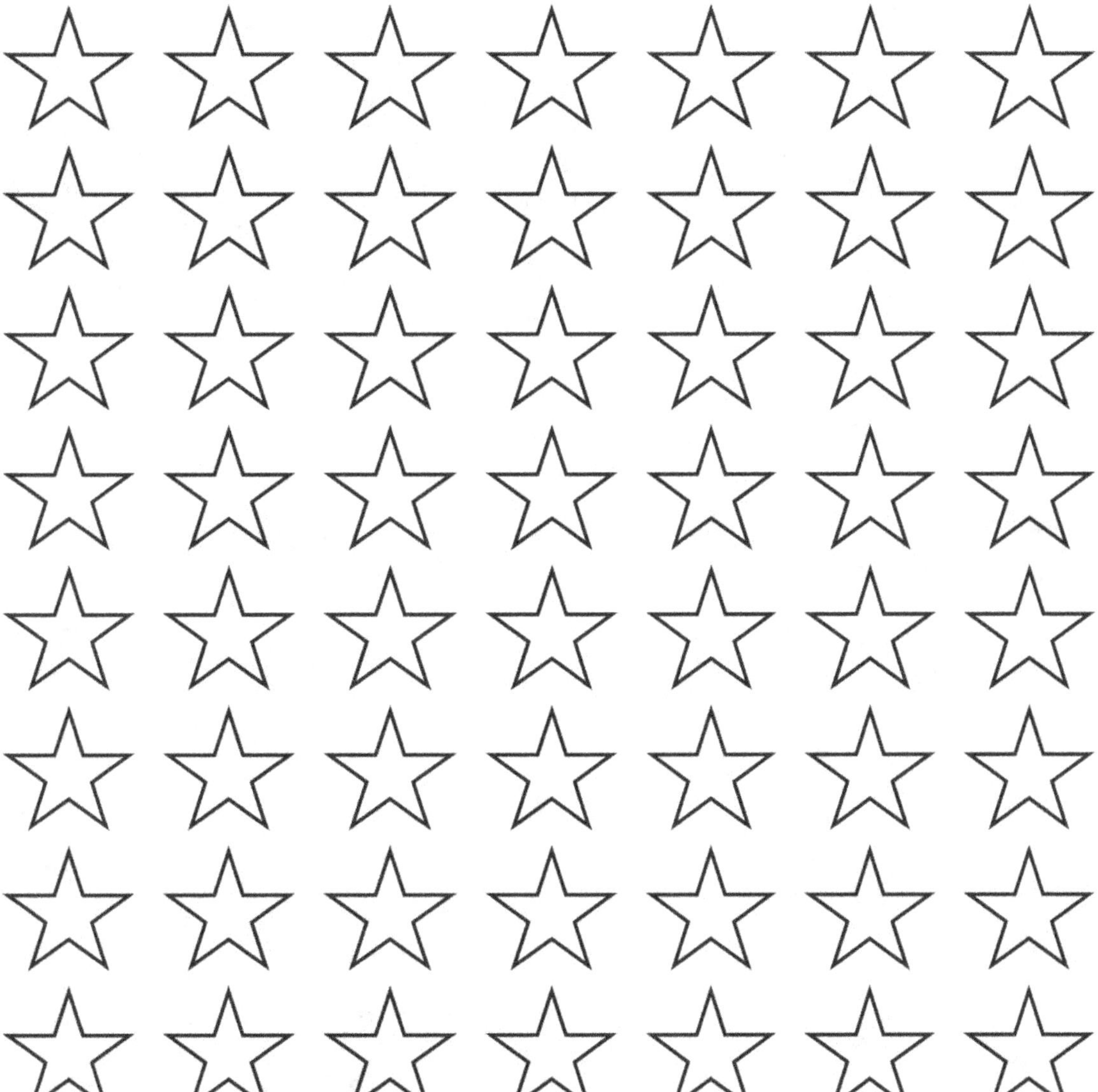

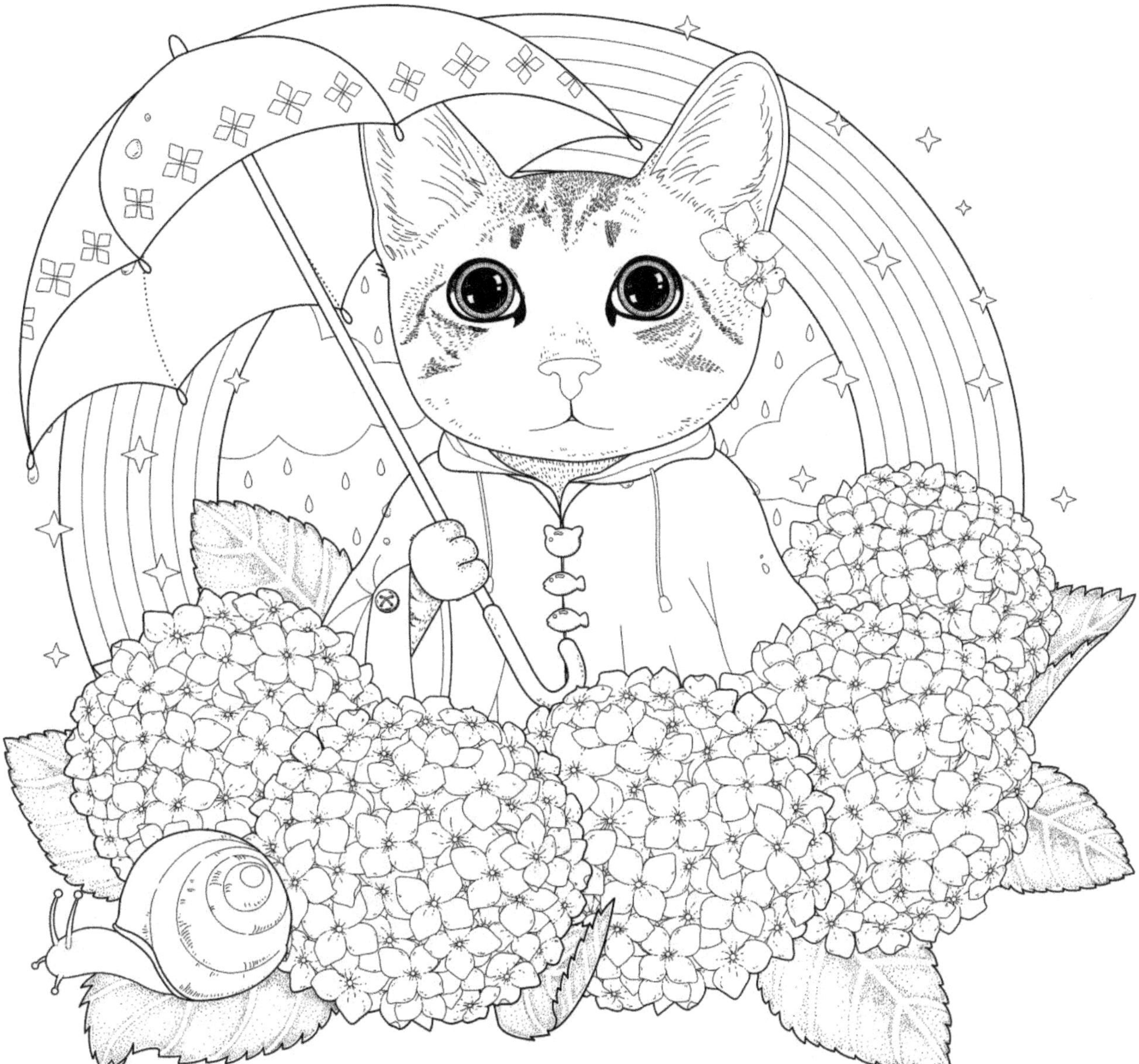

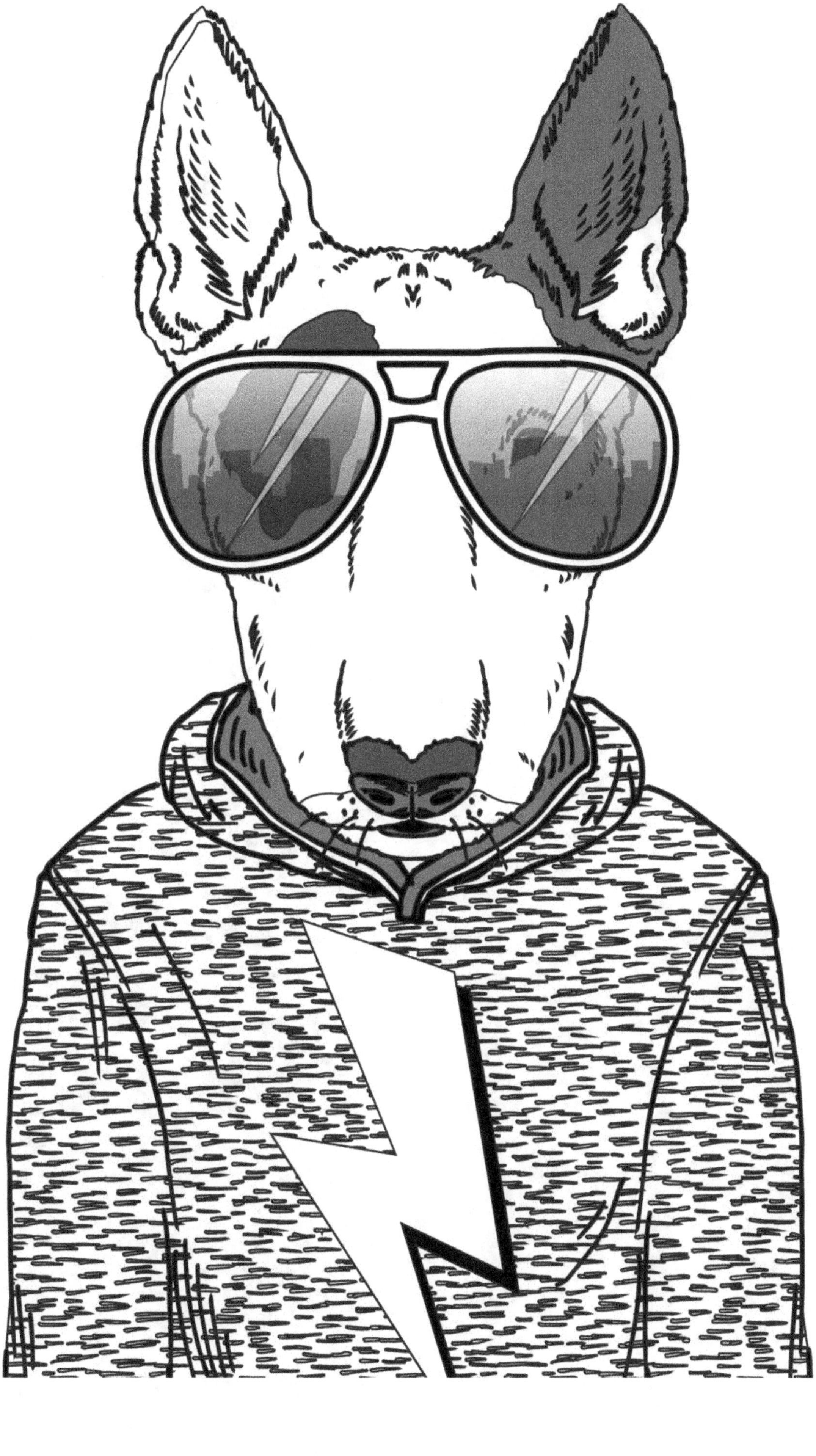

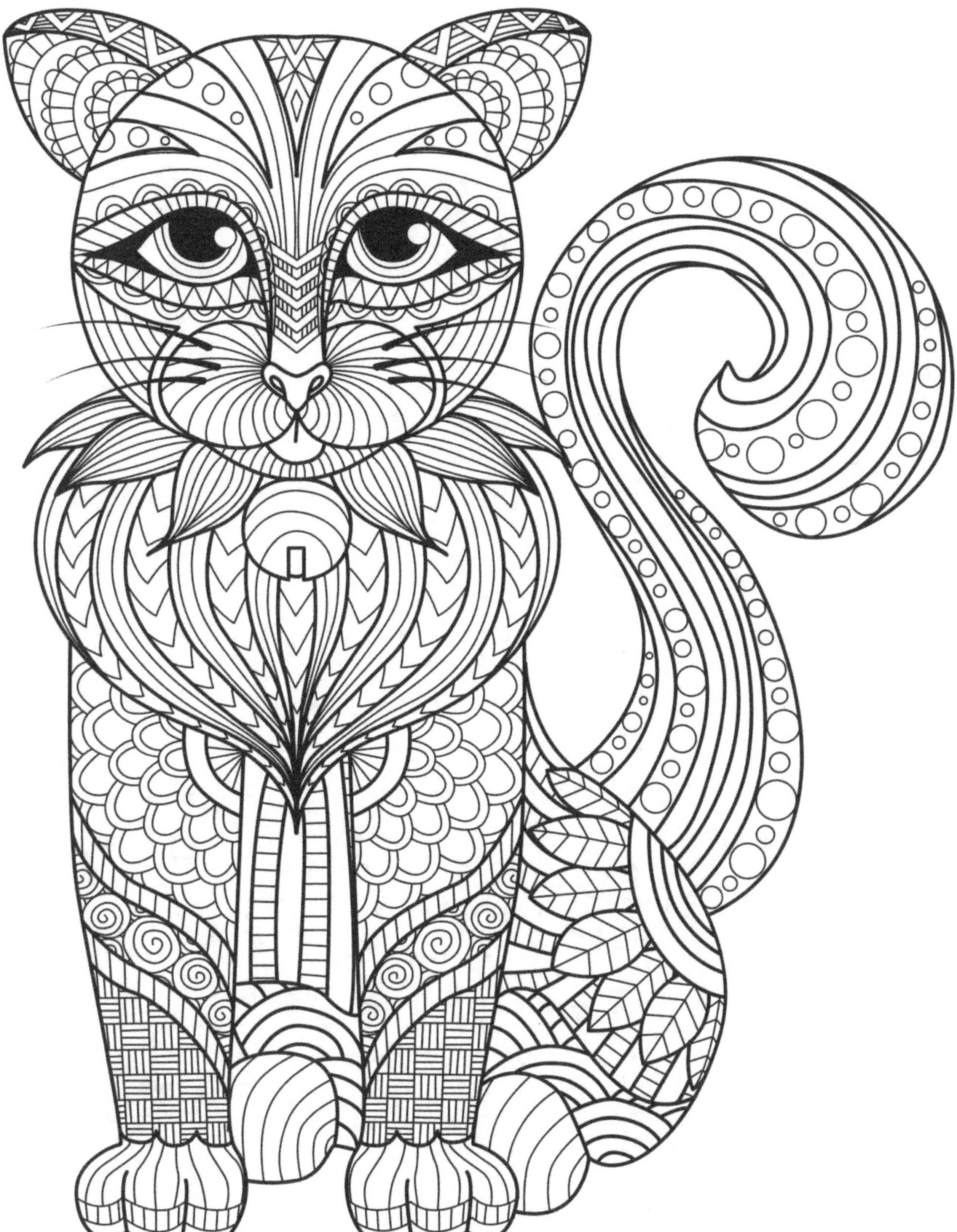

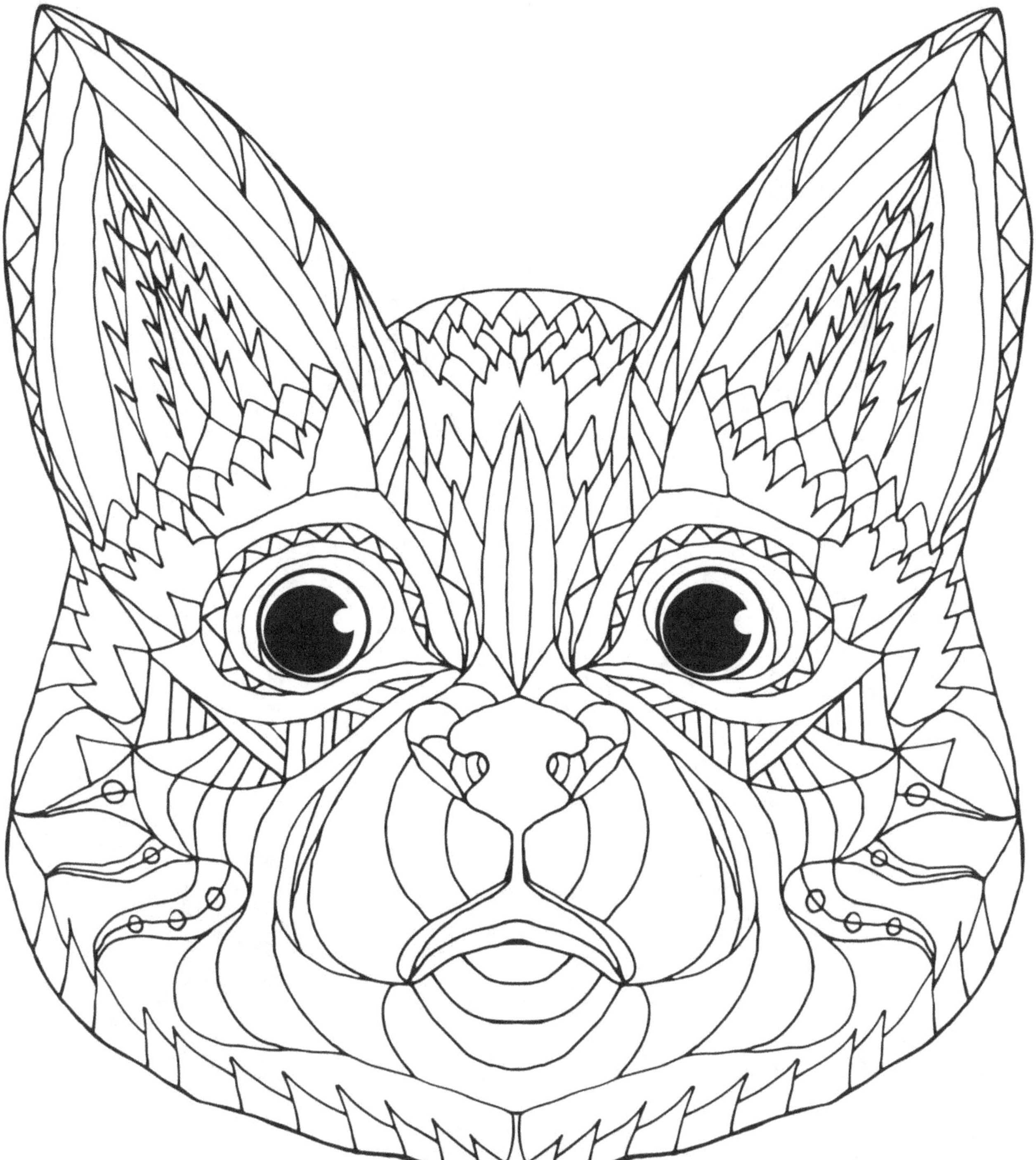

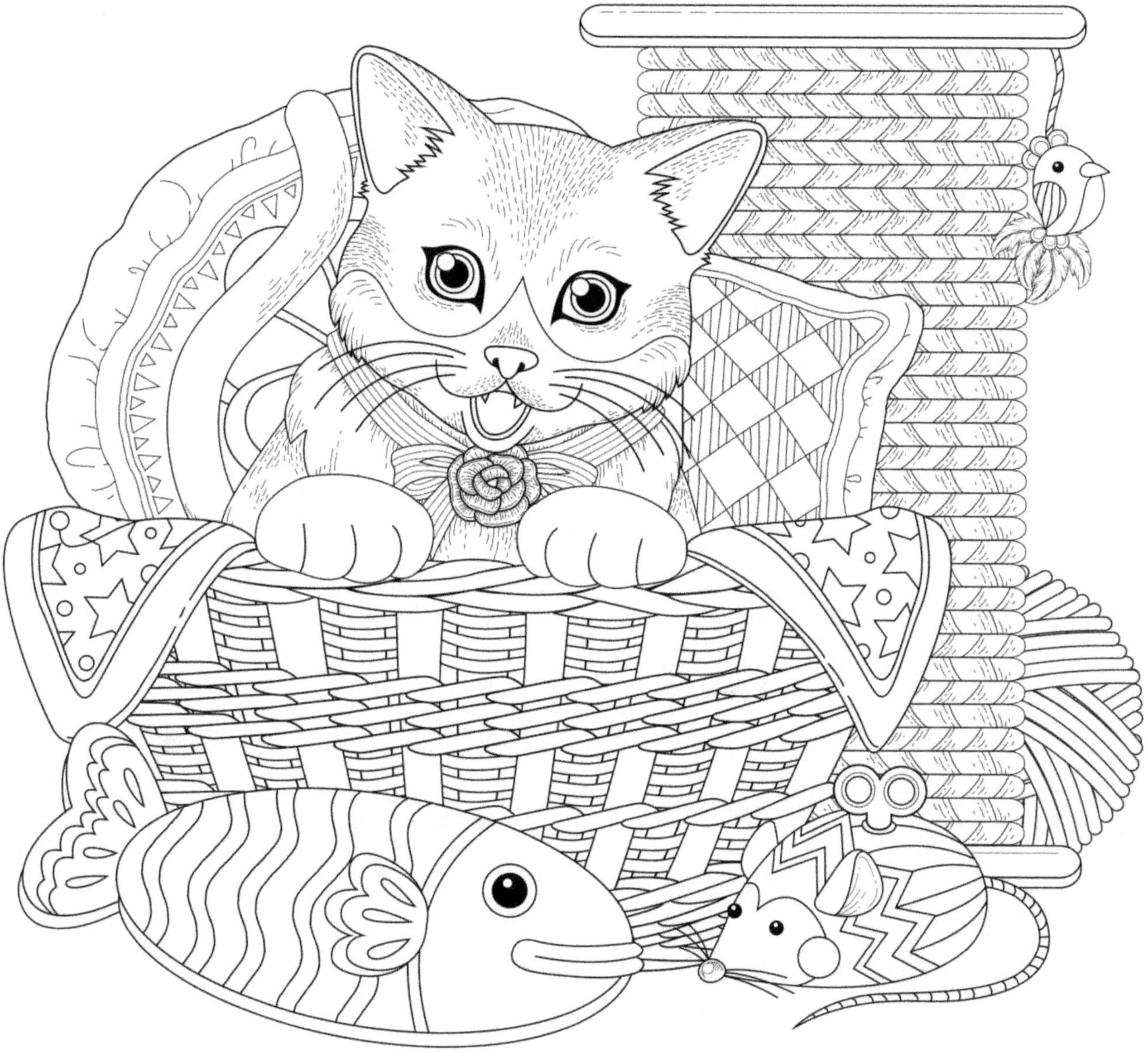

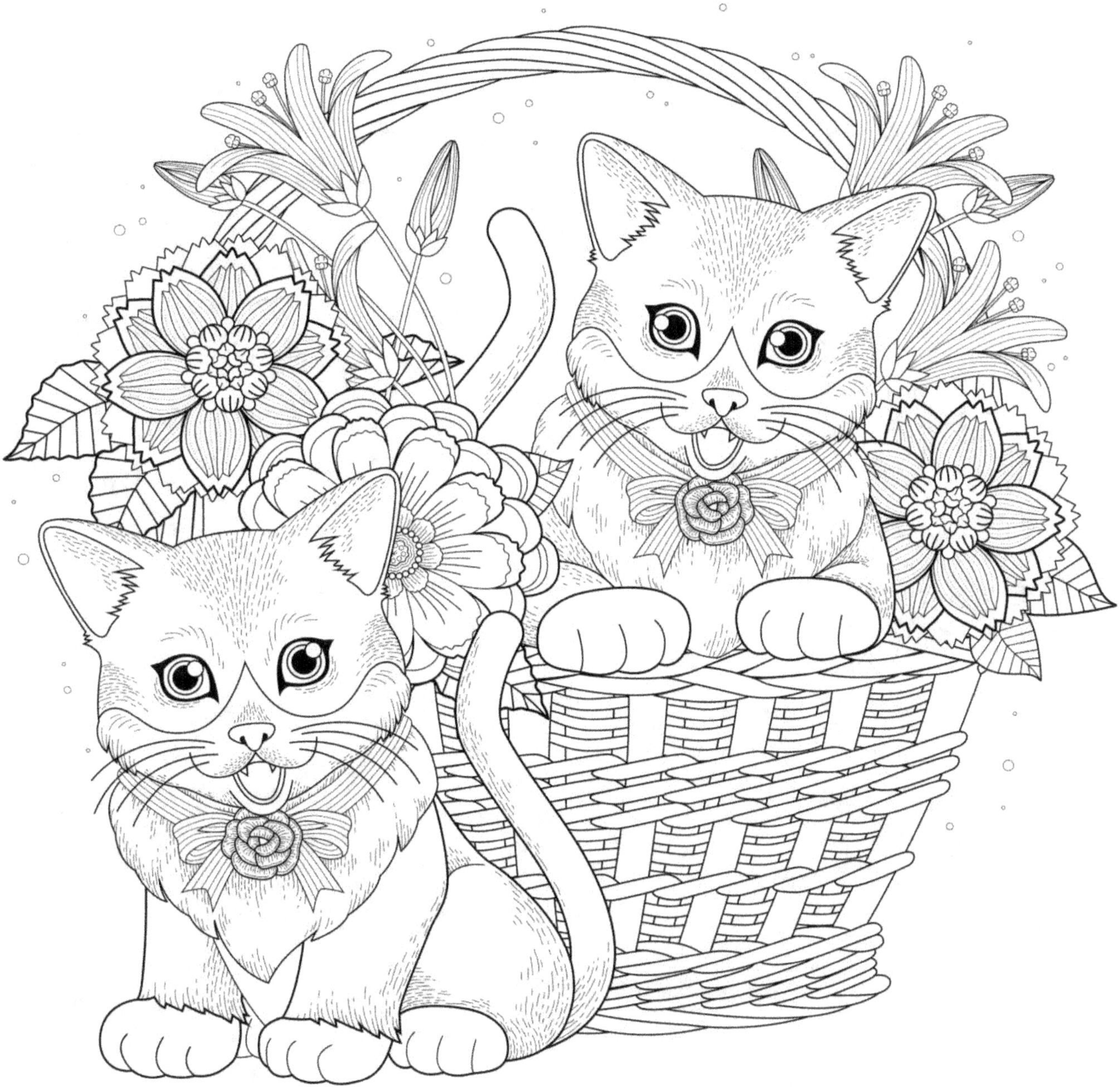

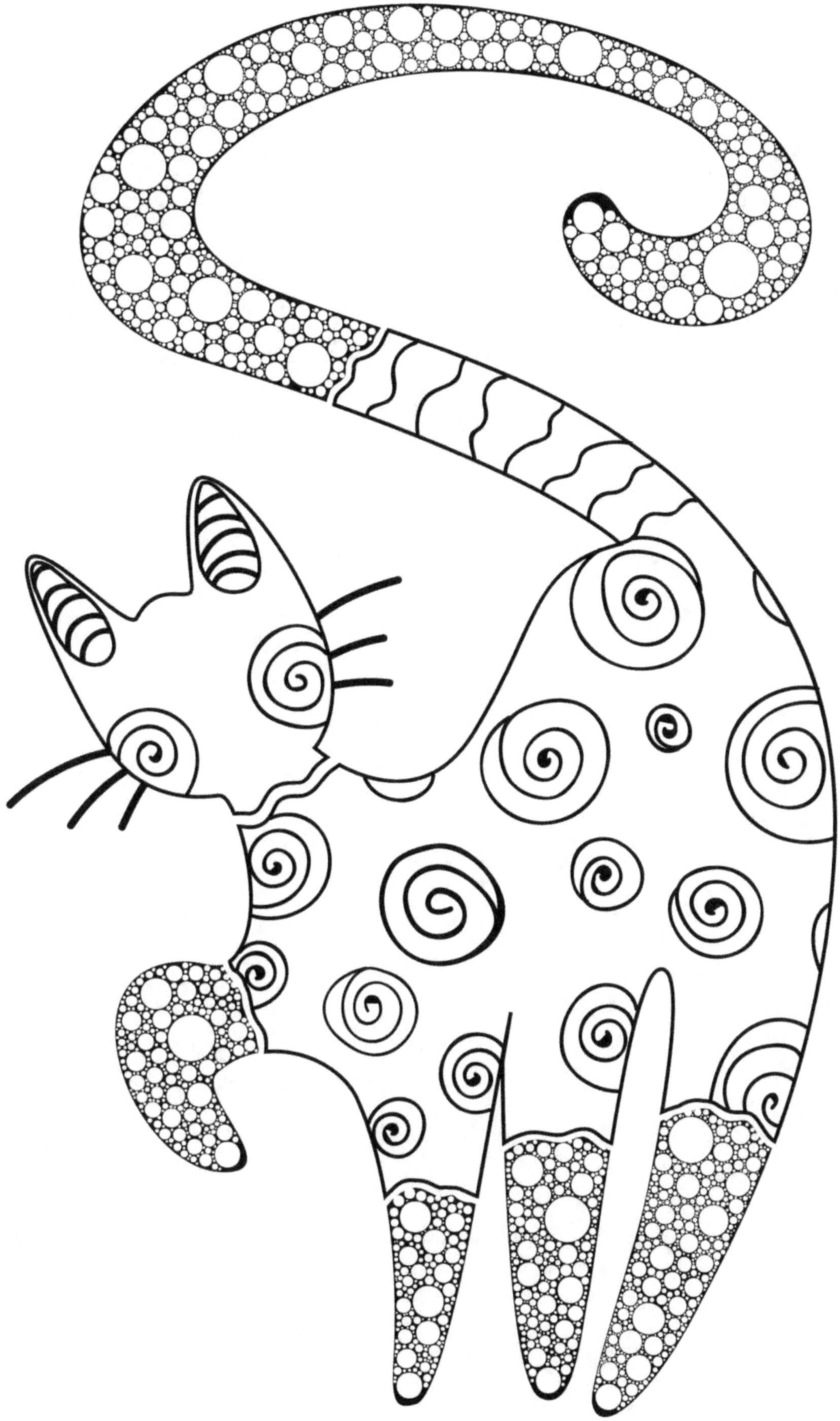

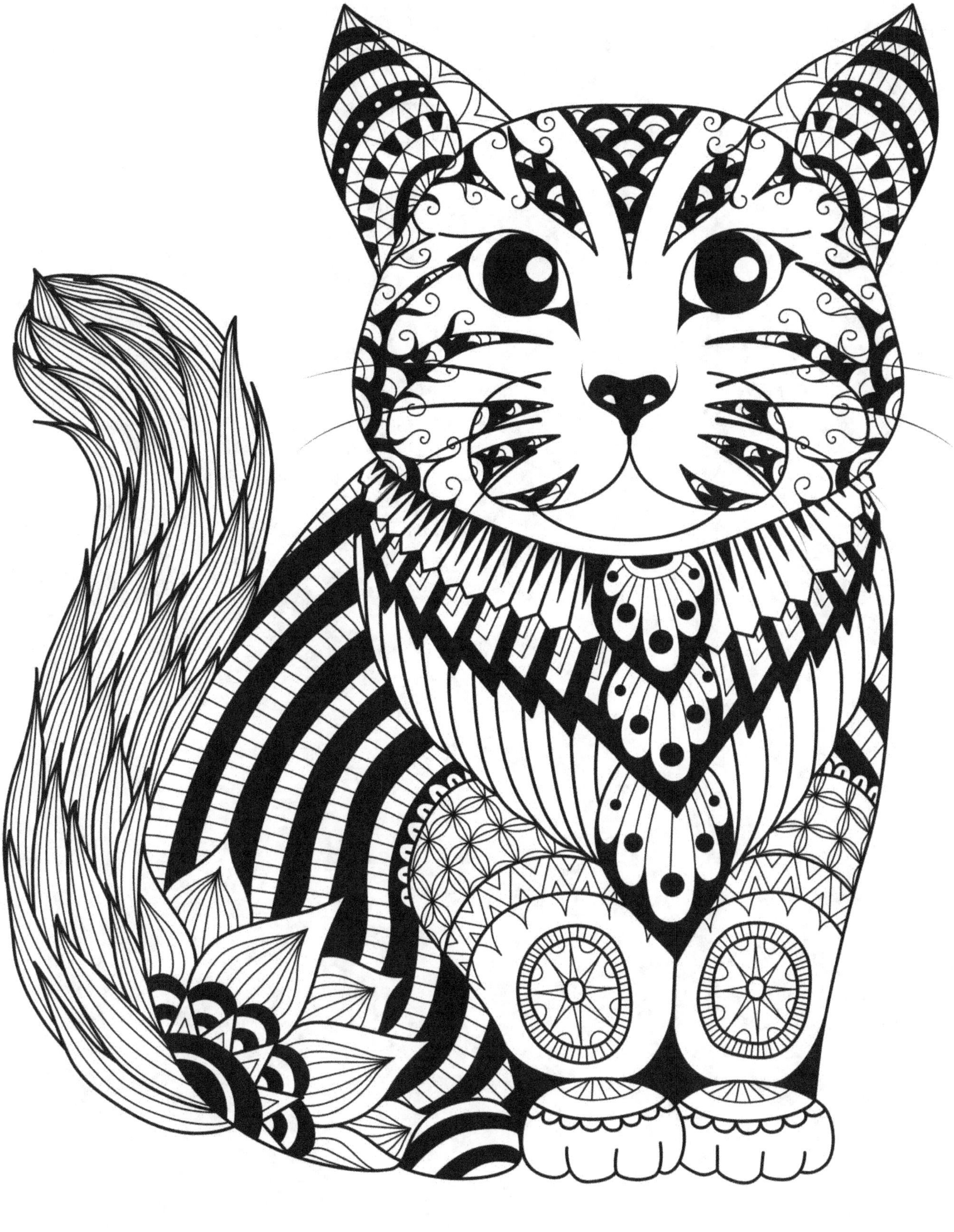

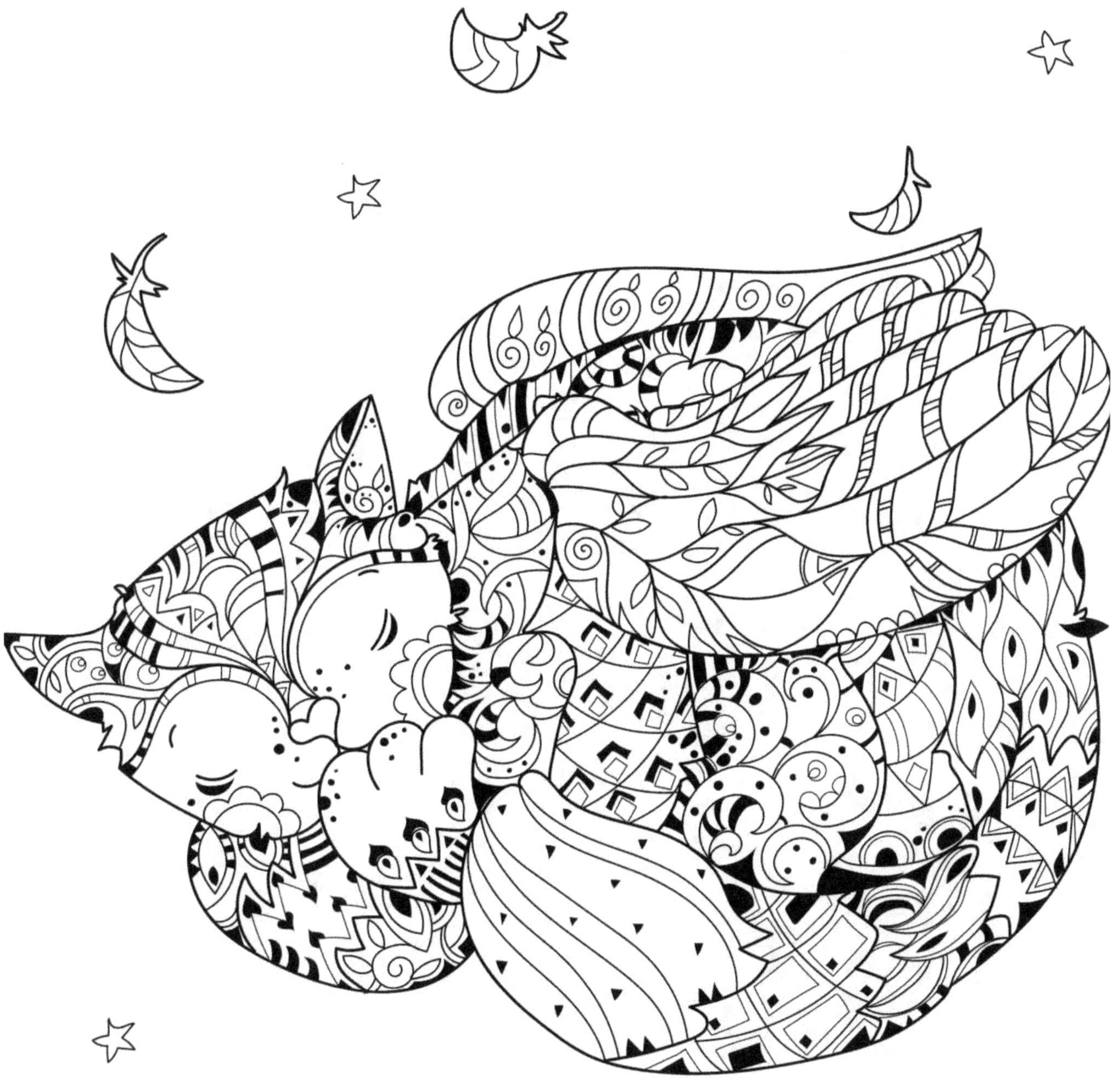

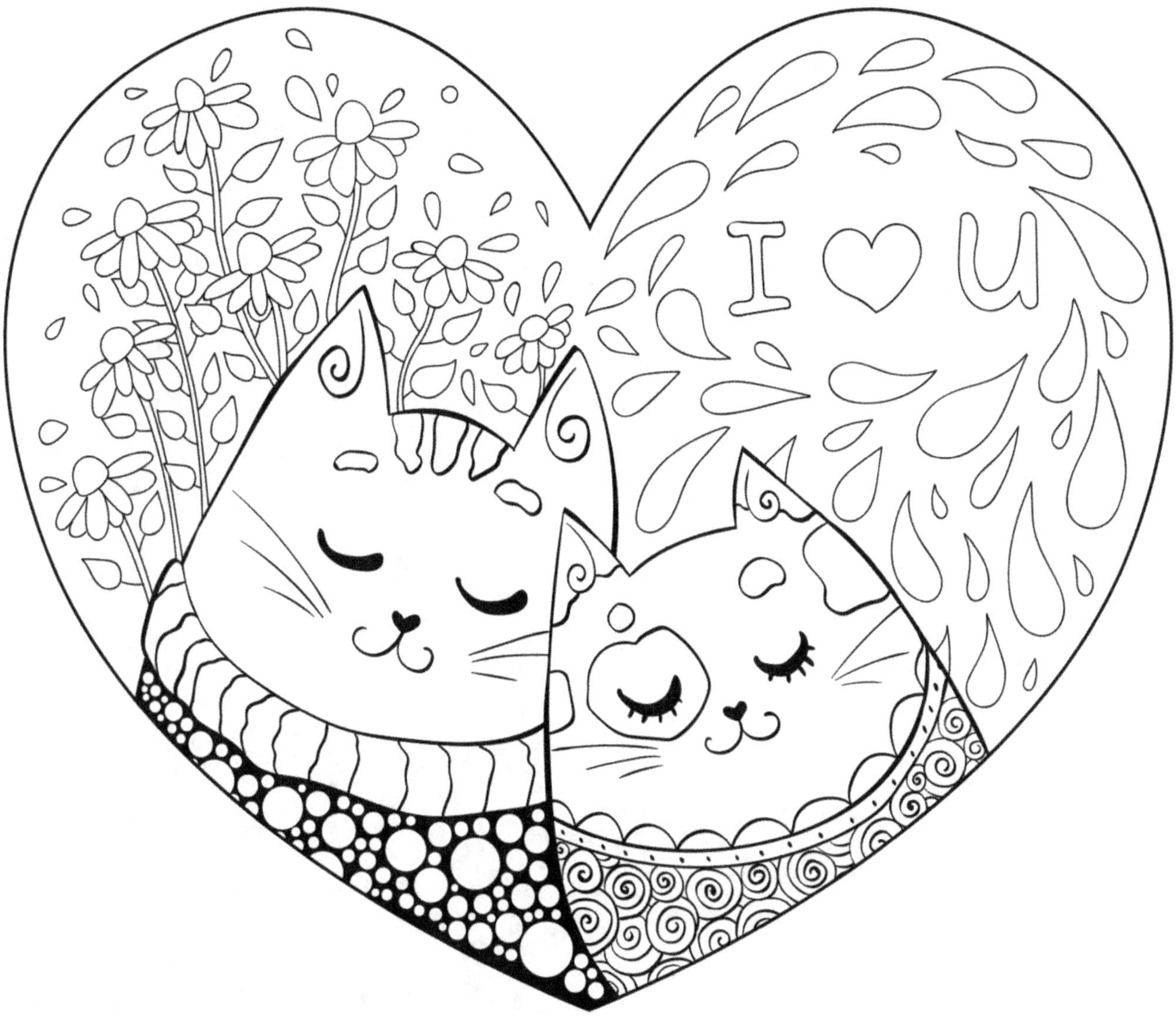
I ♥ U

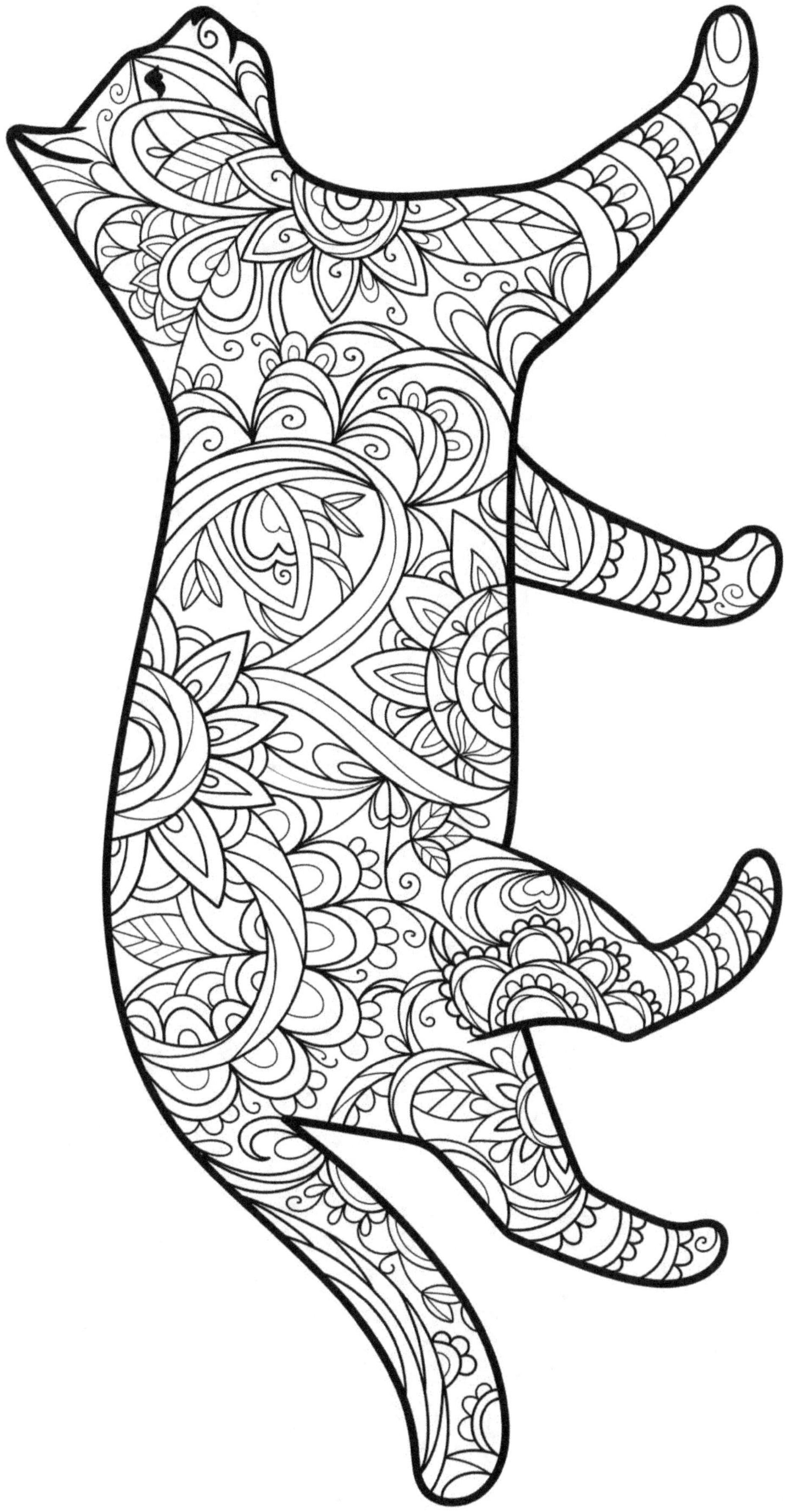

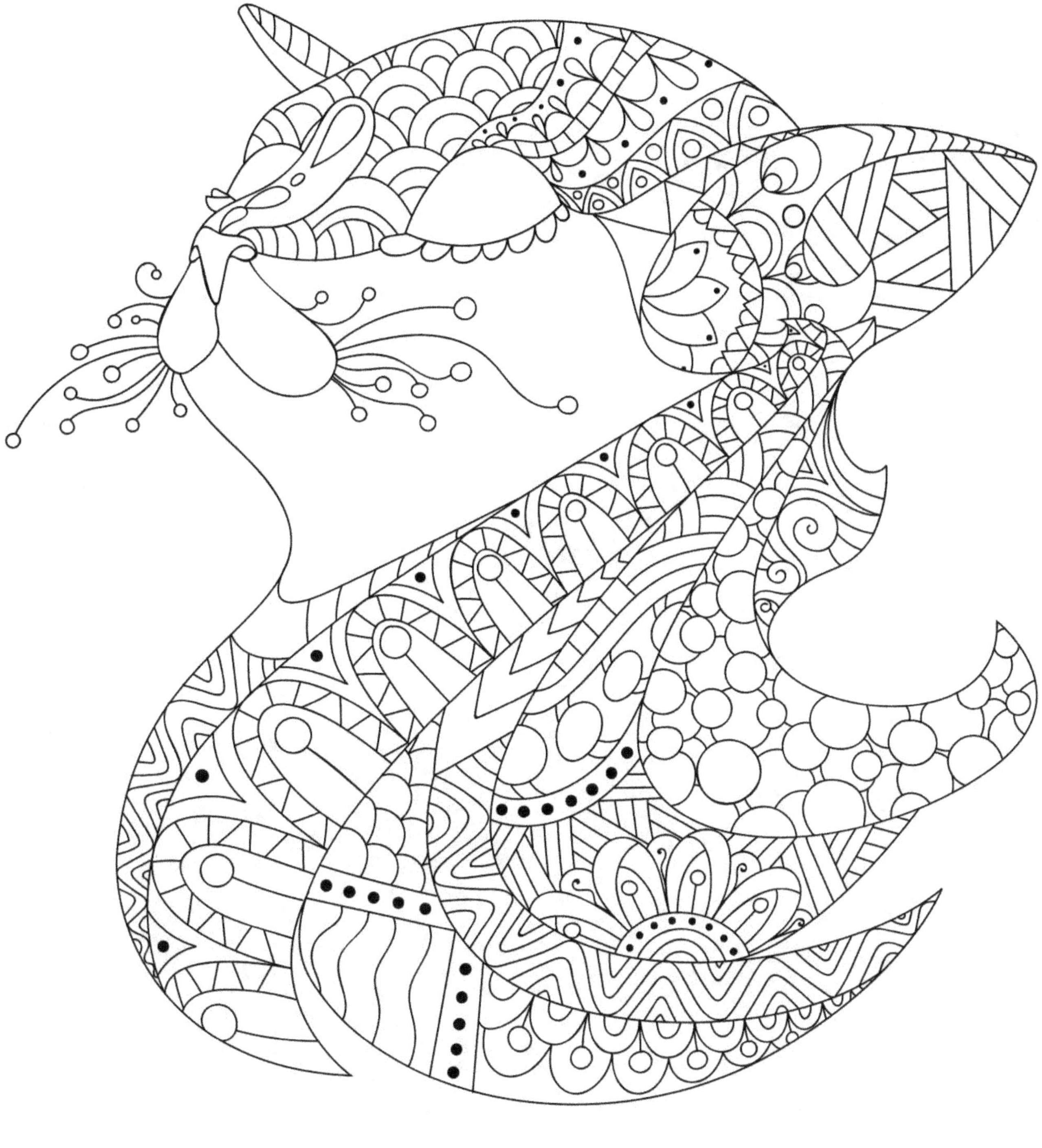

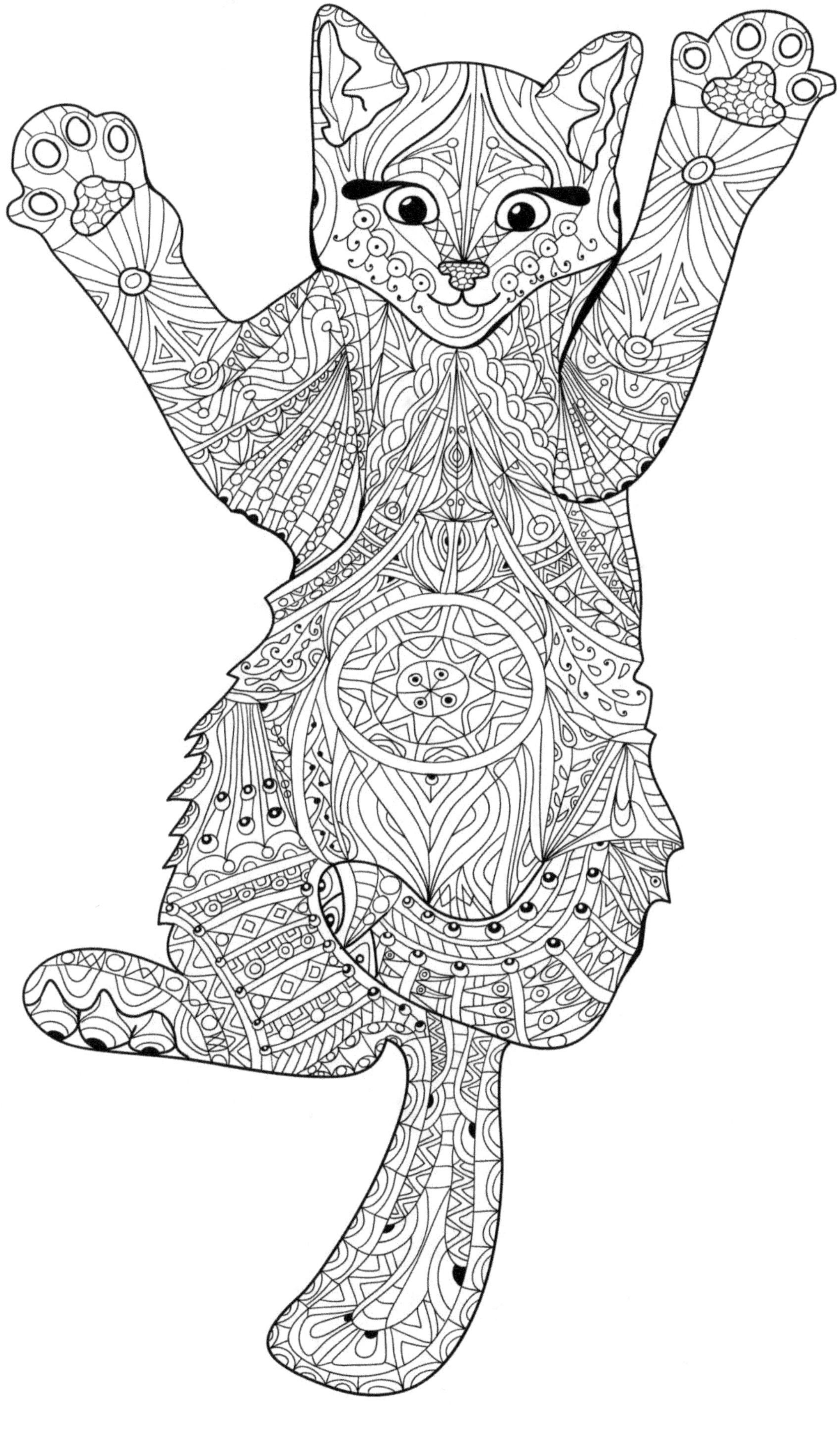

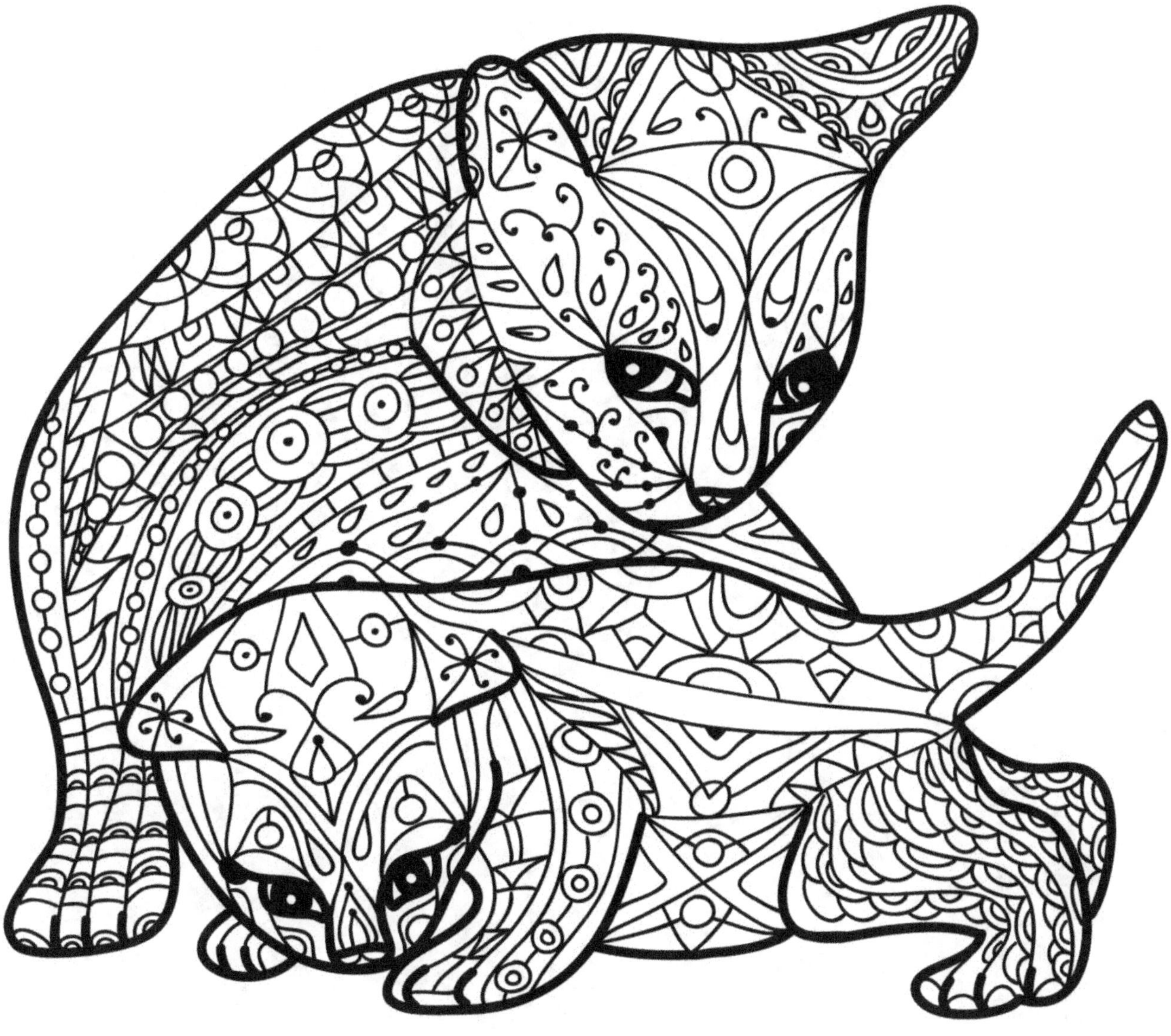

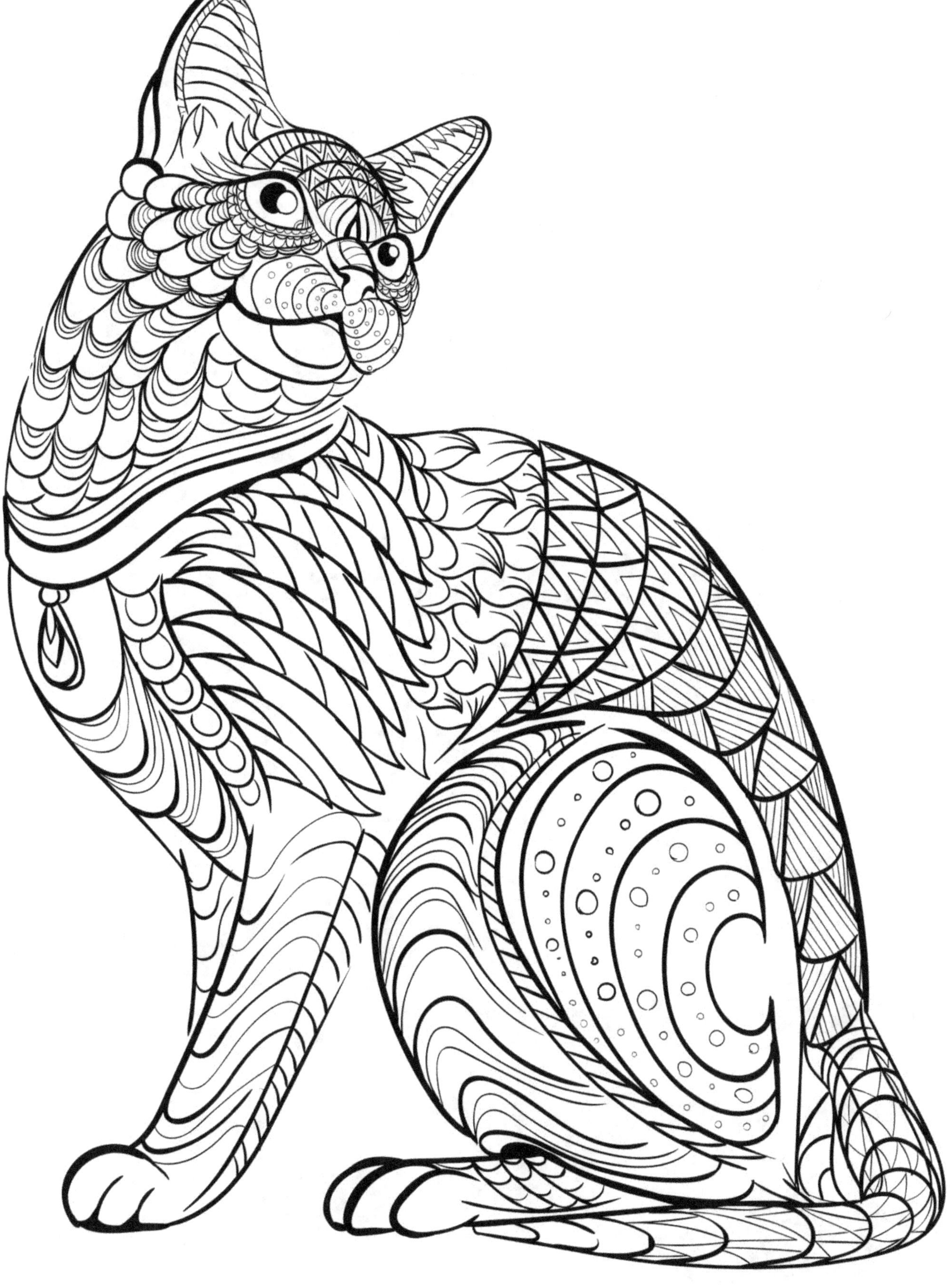

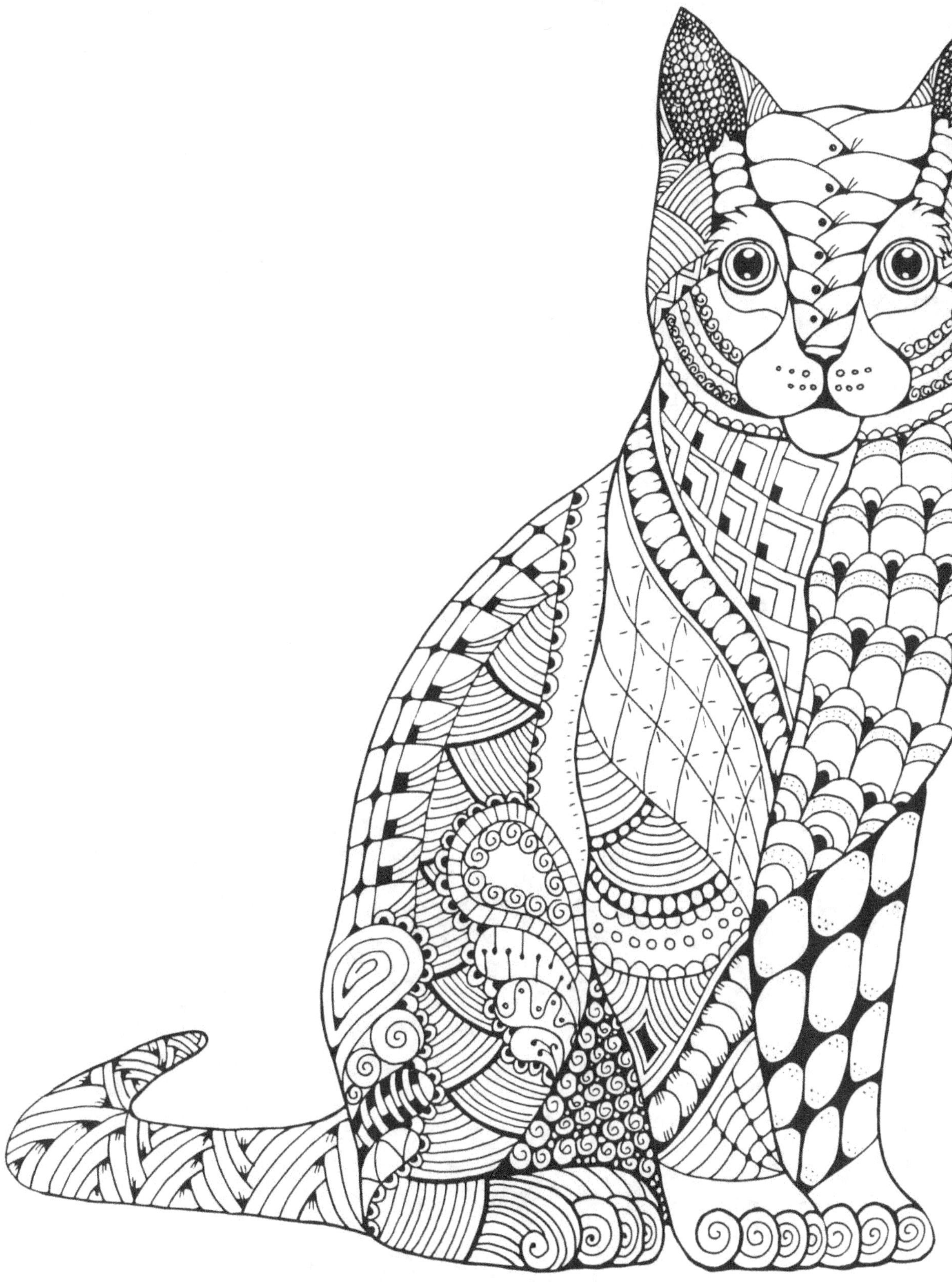

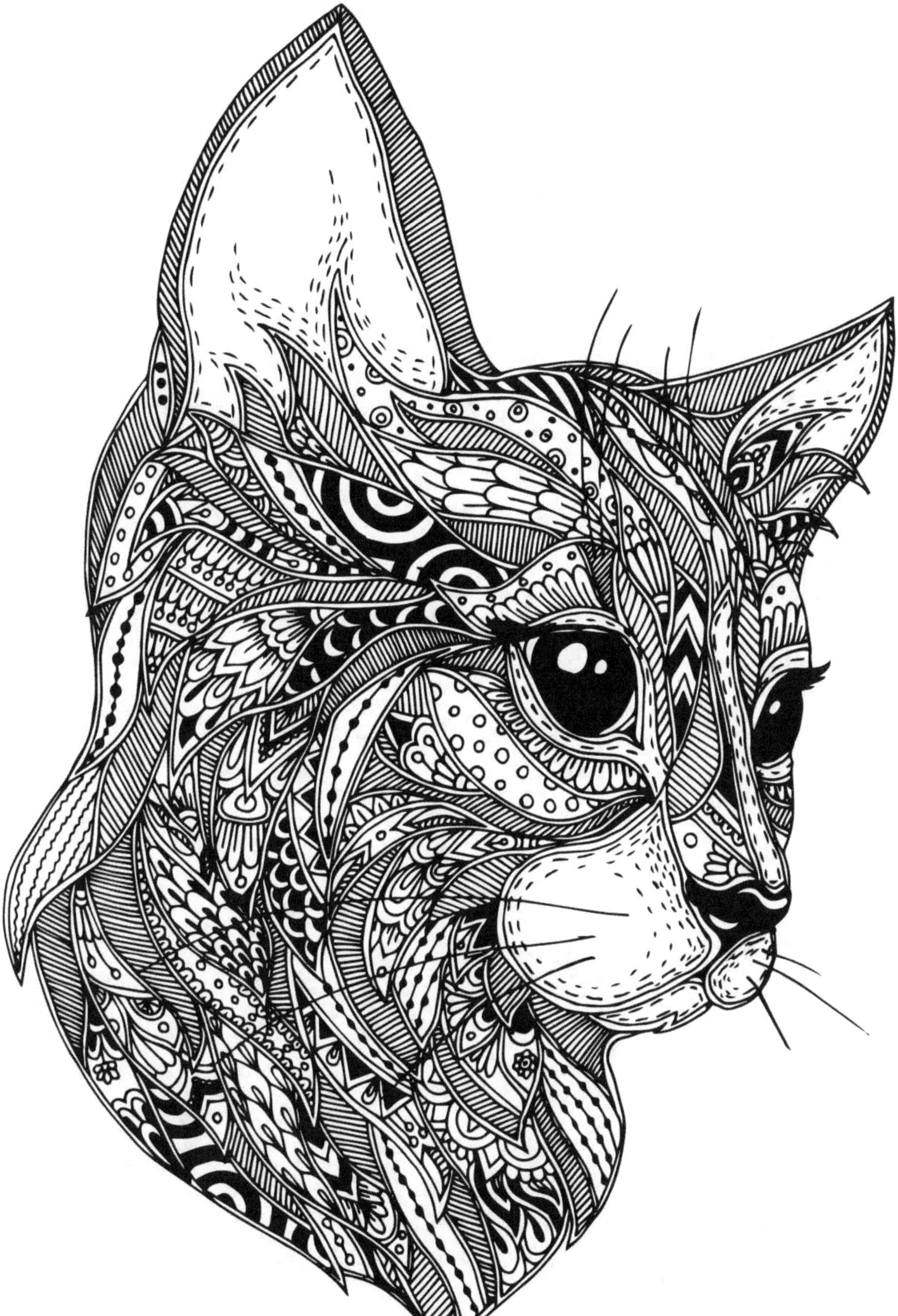

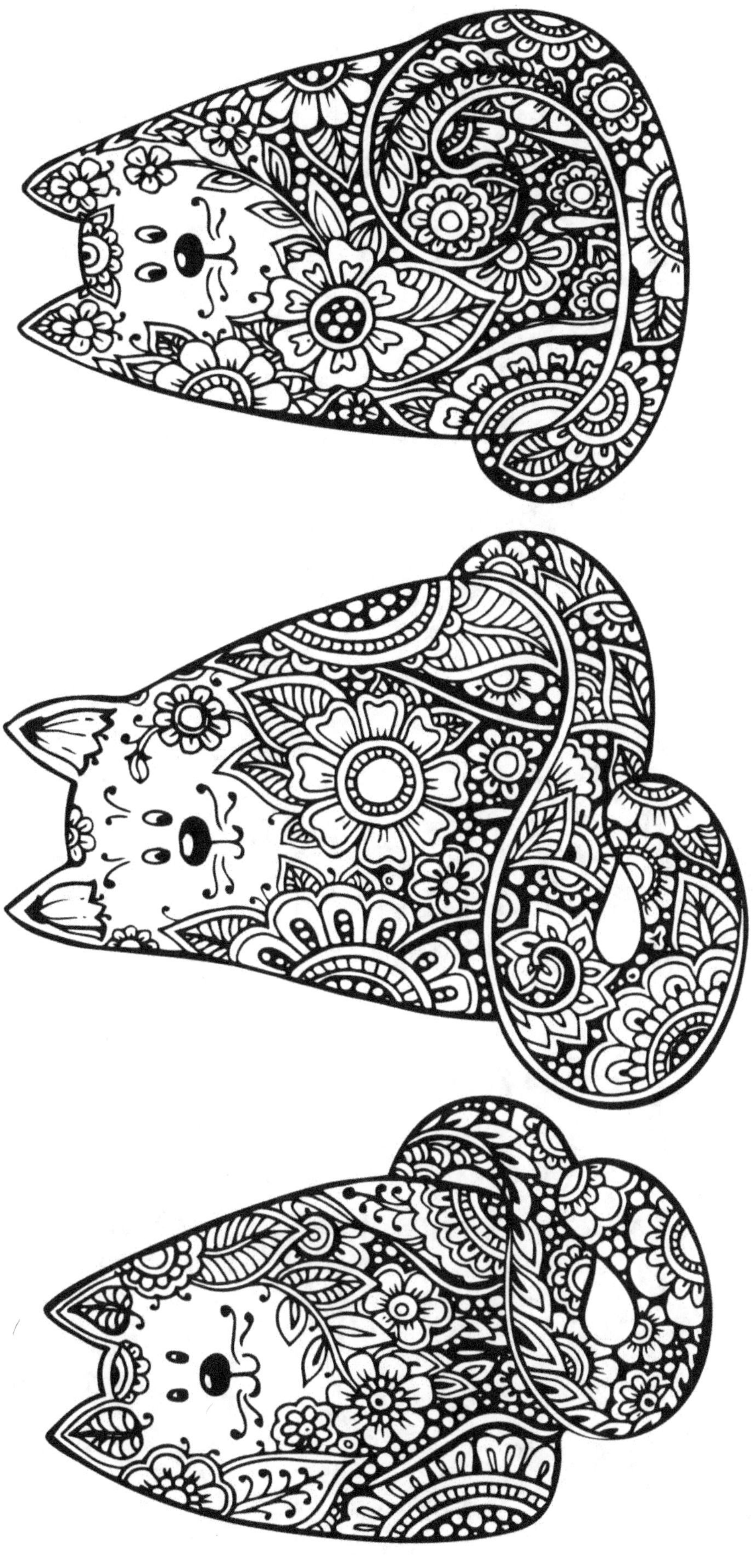

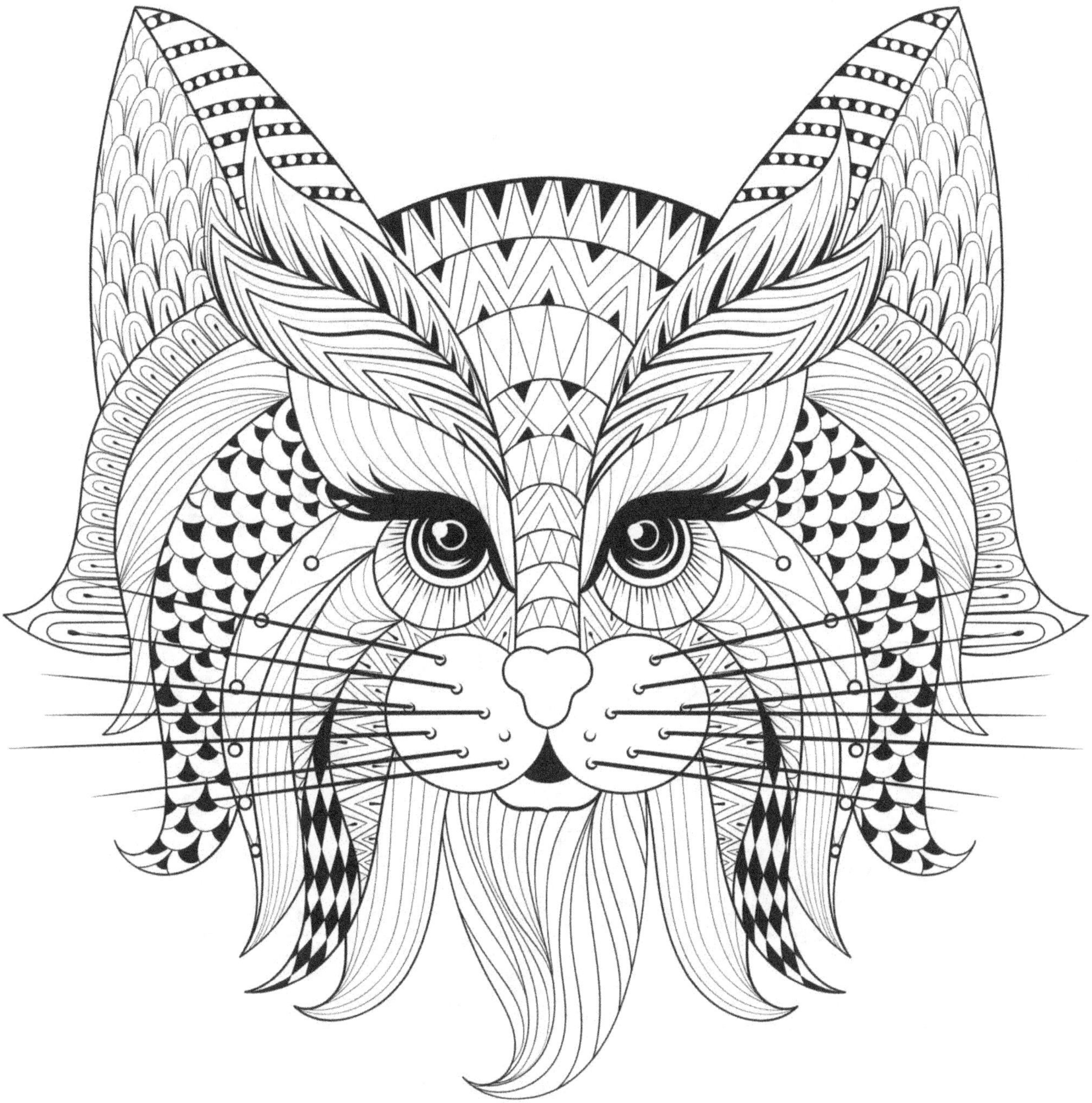

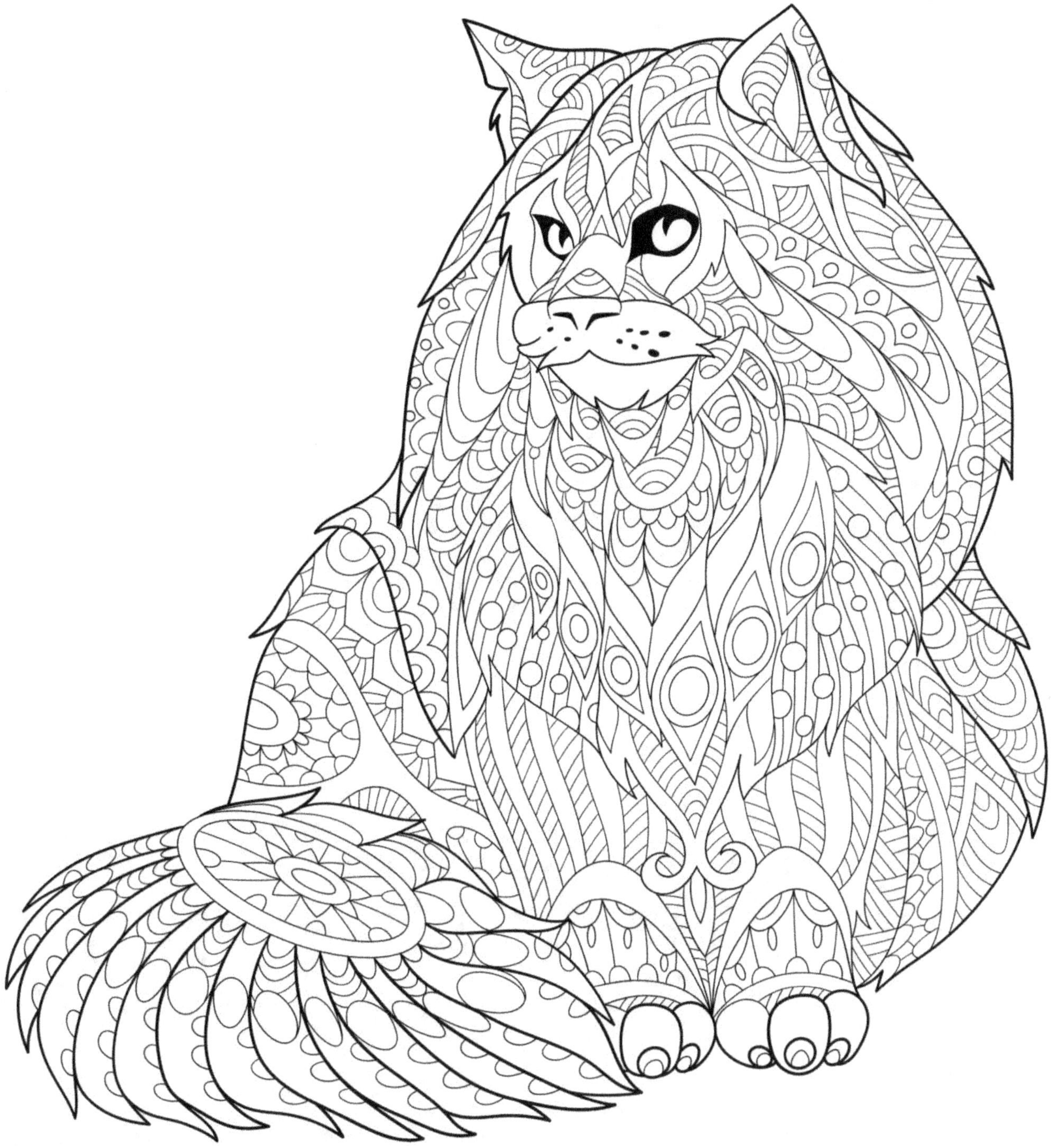

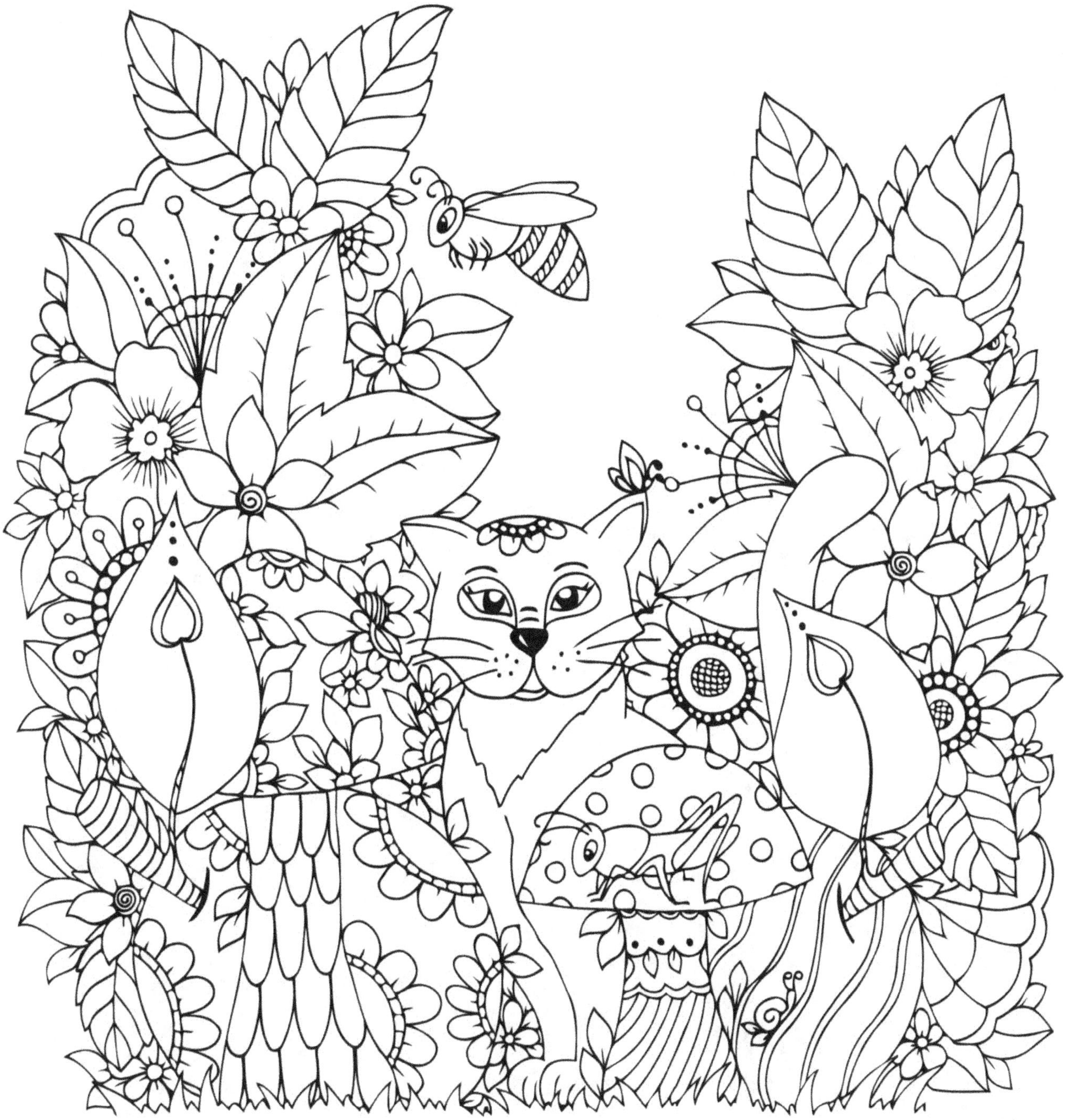

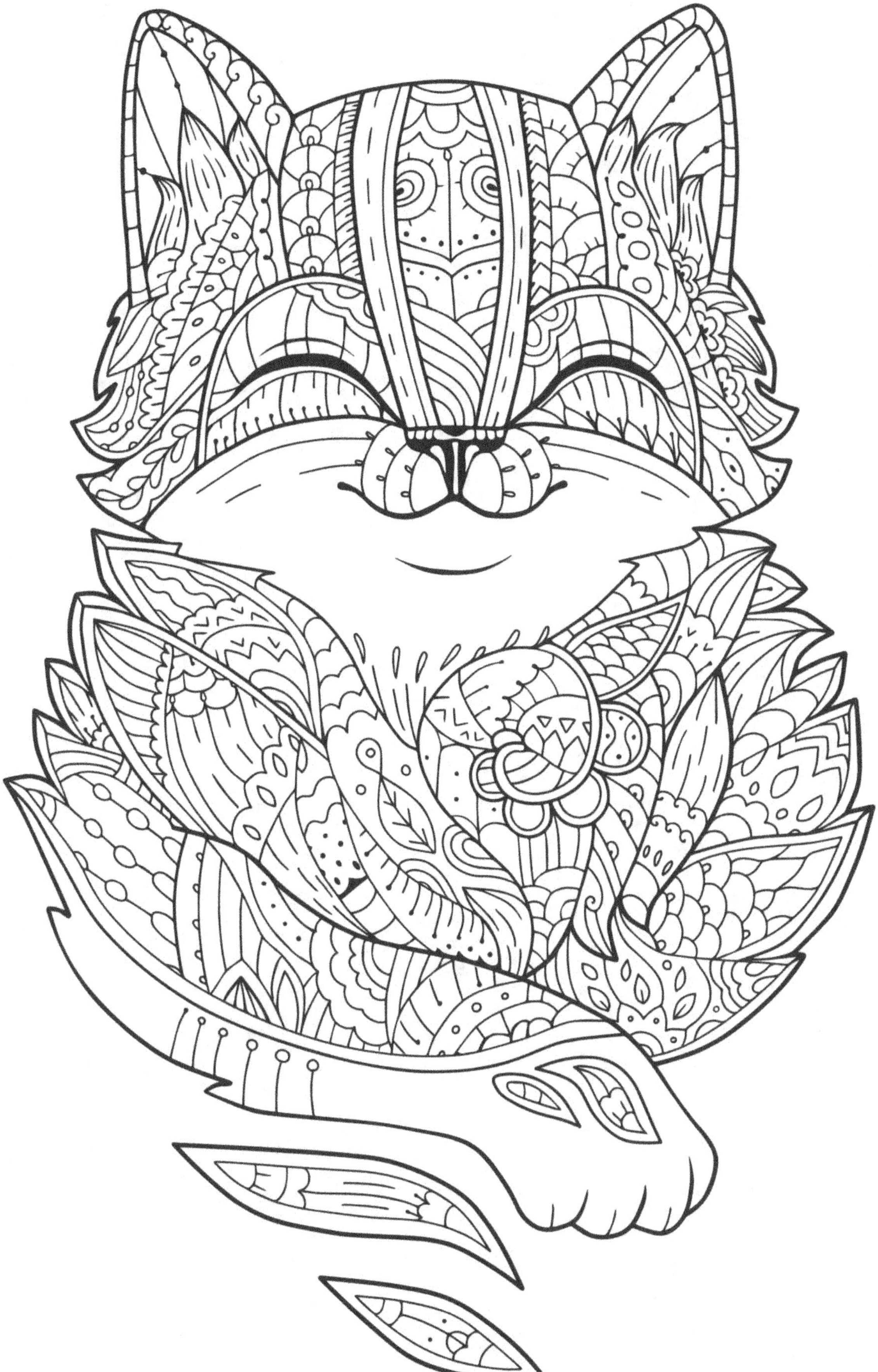

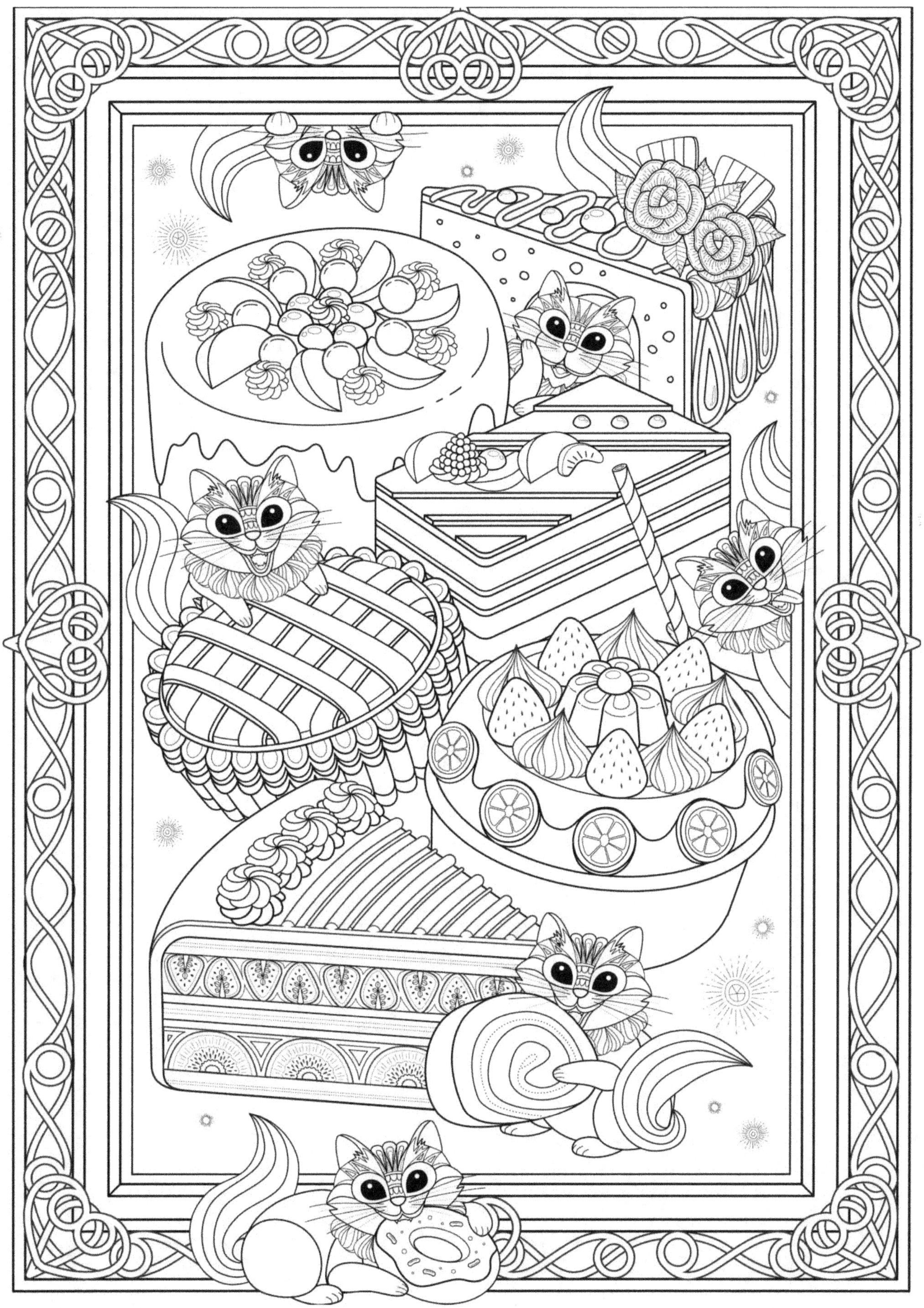

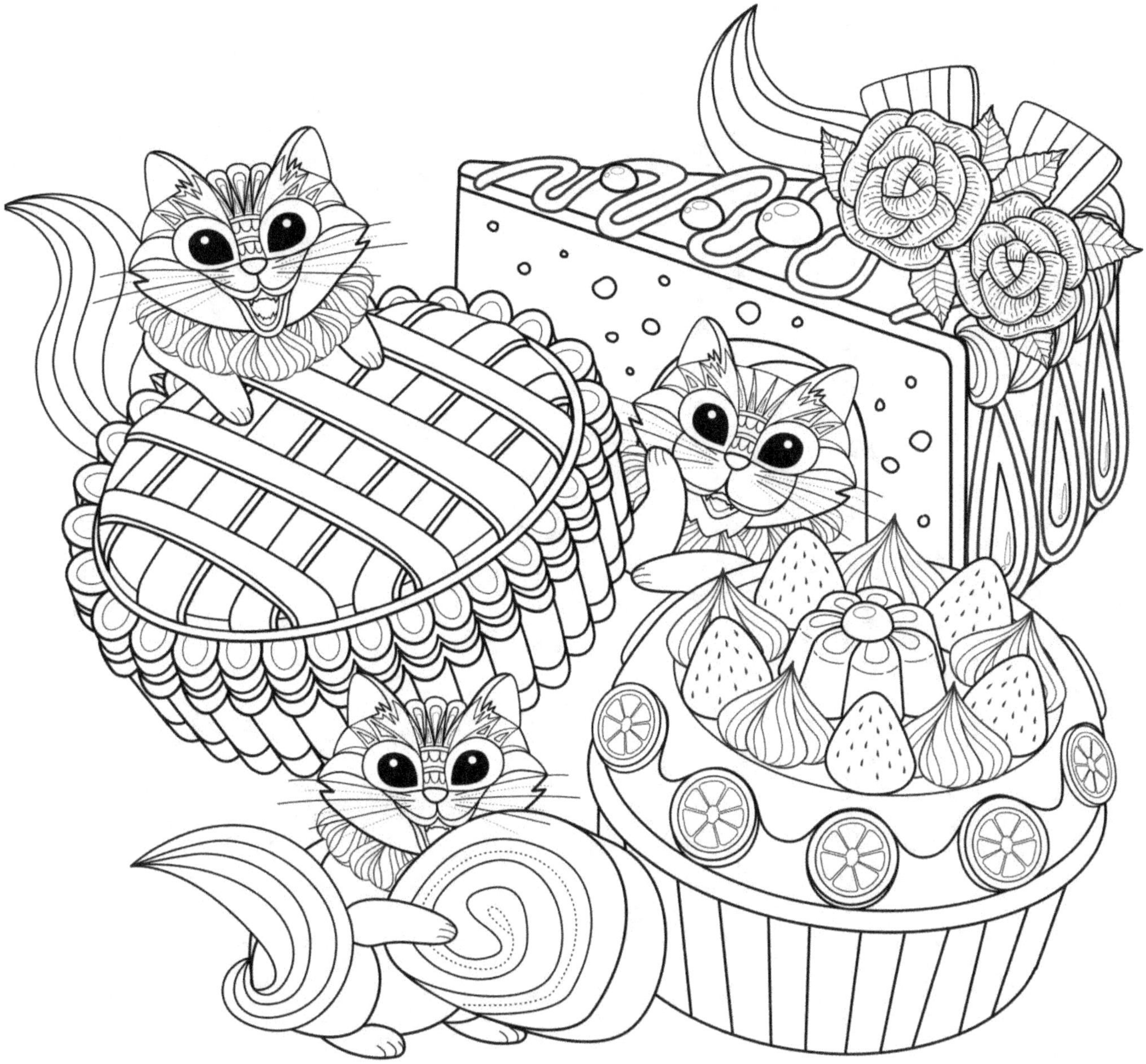

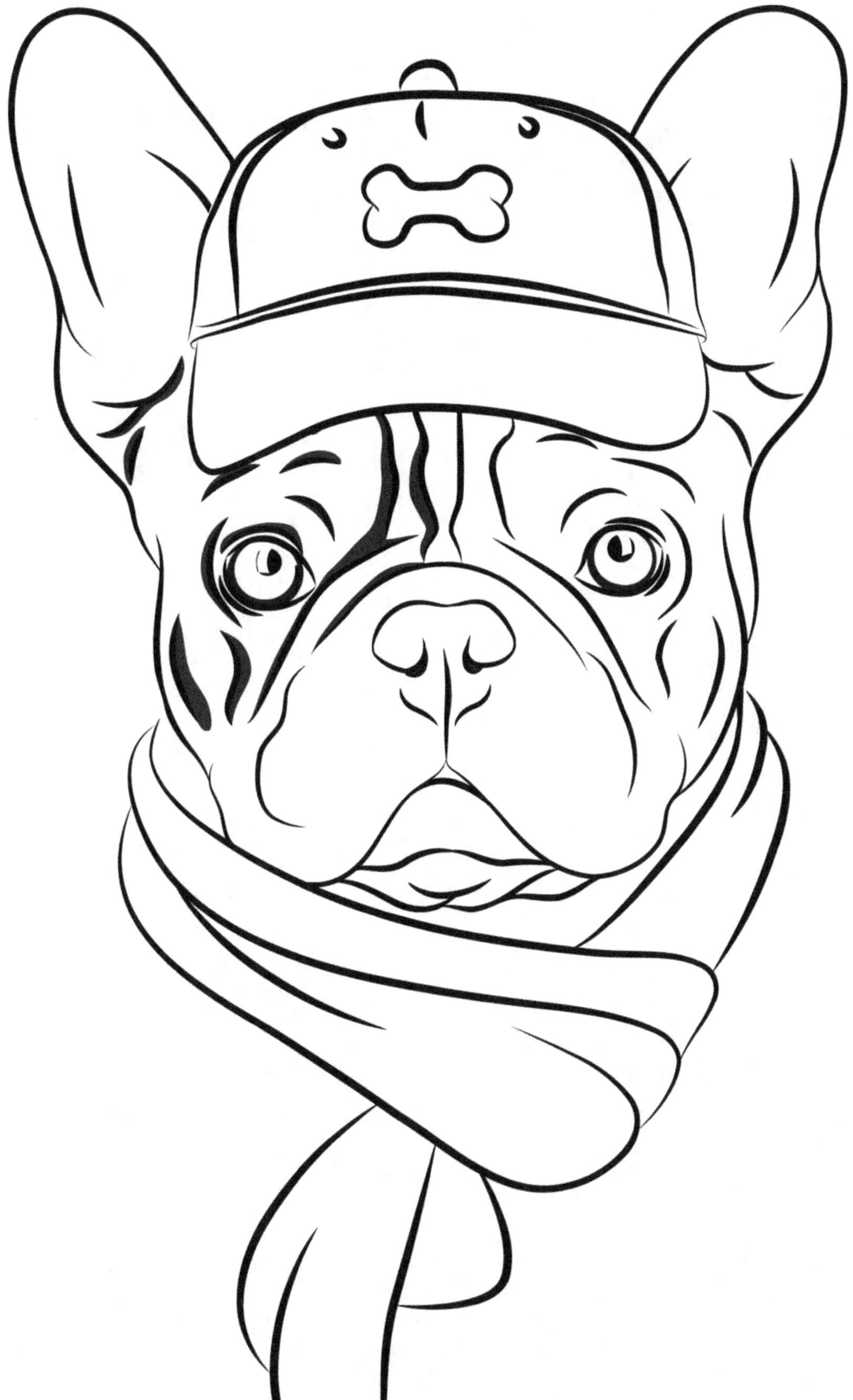

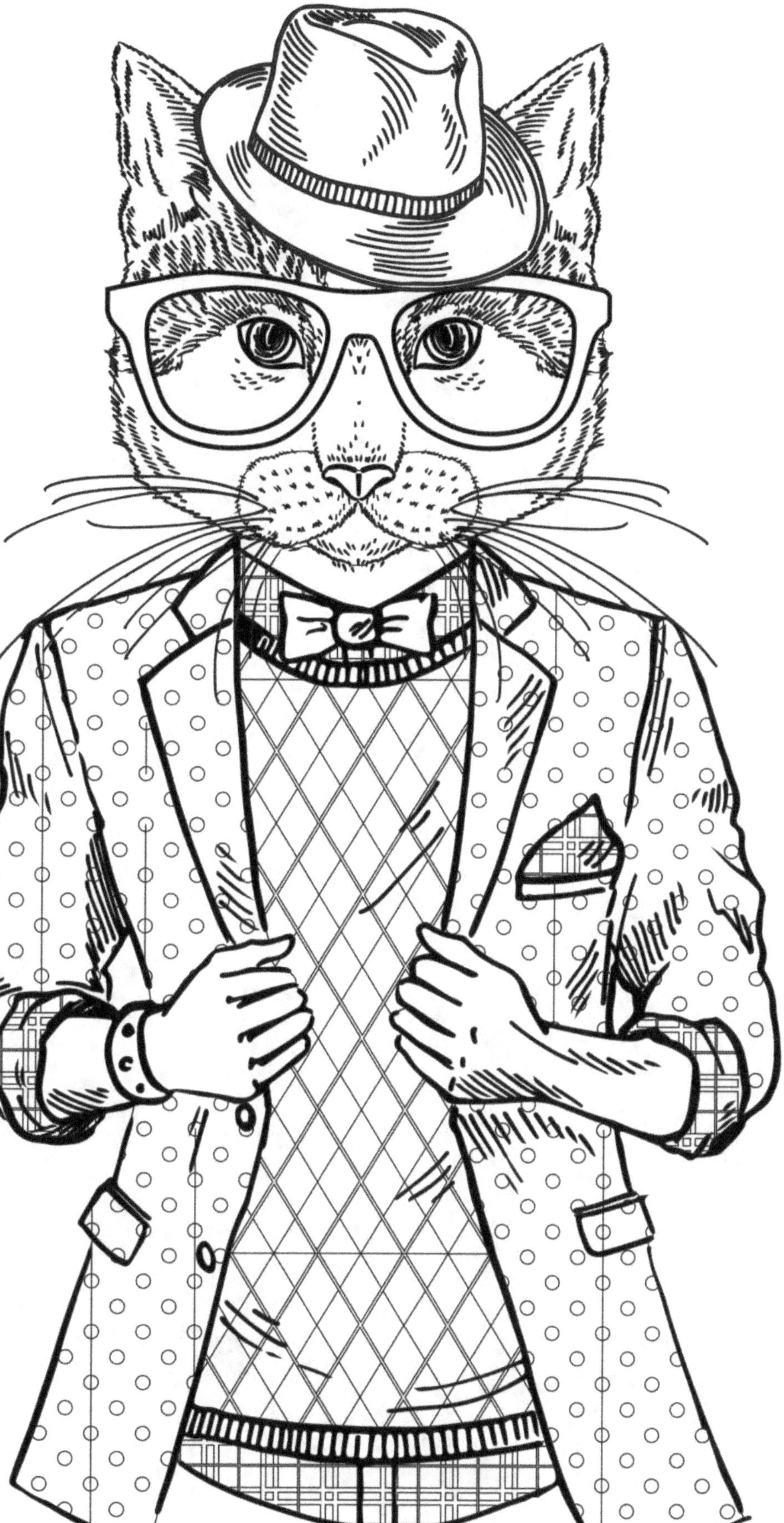

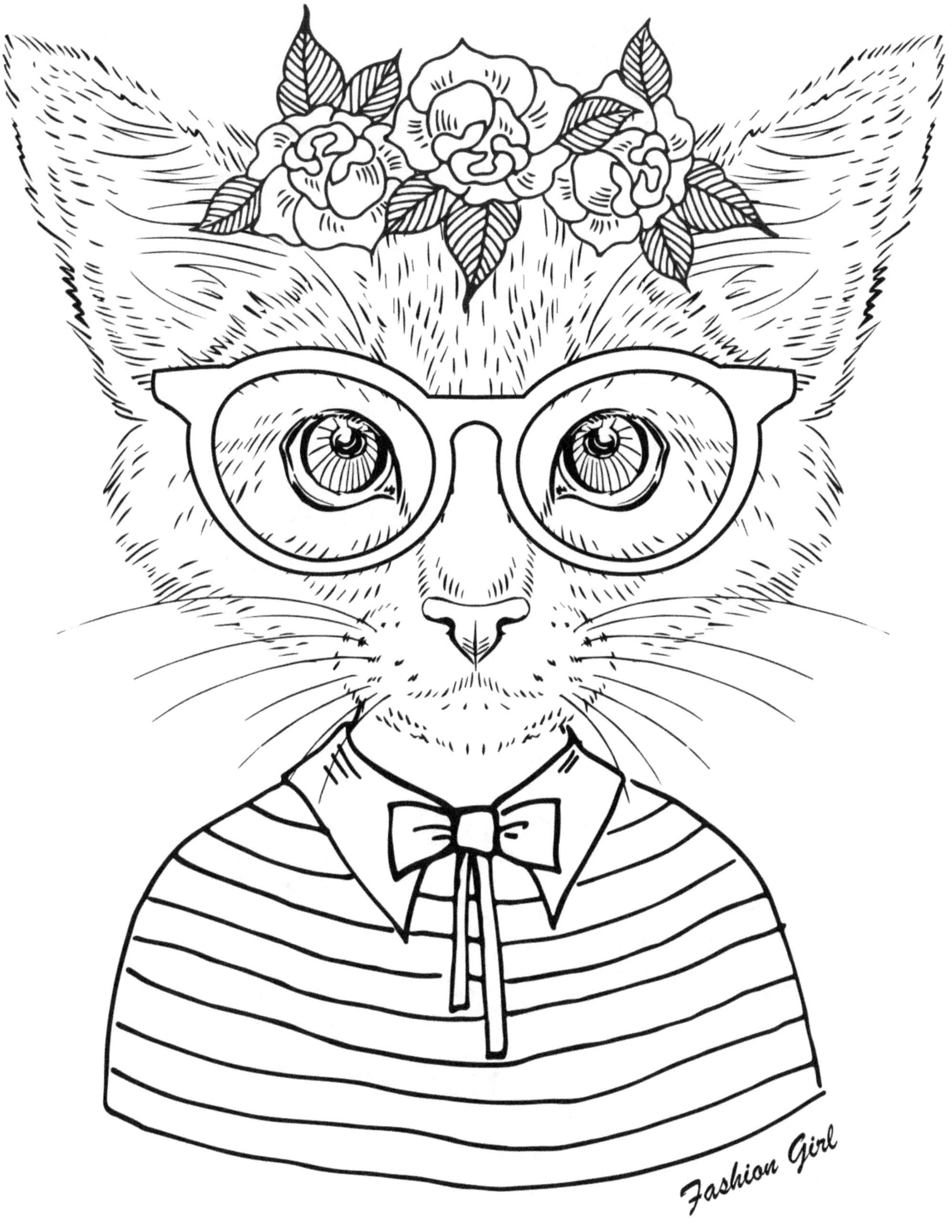
Fashion Girl

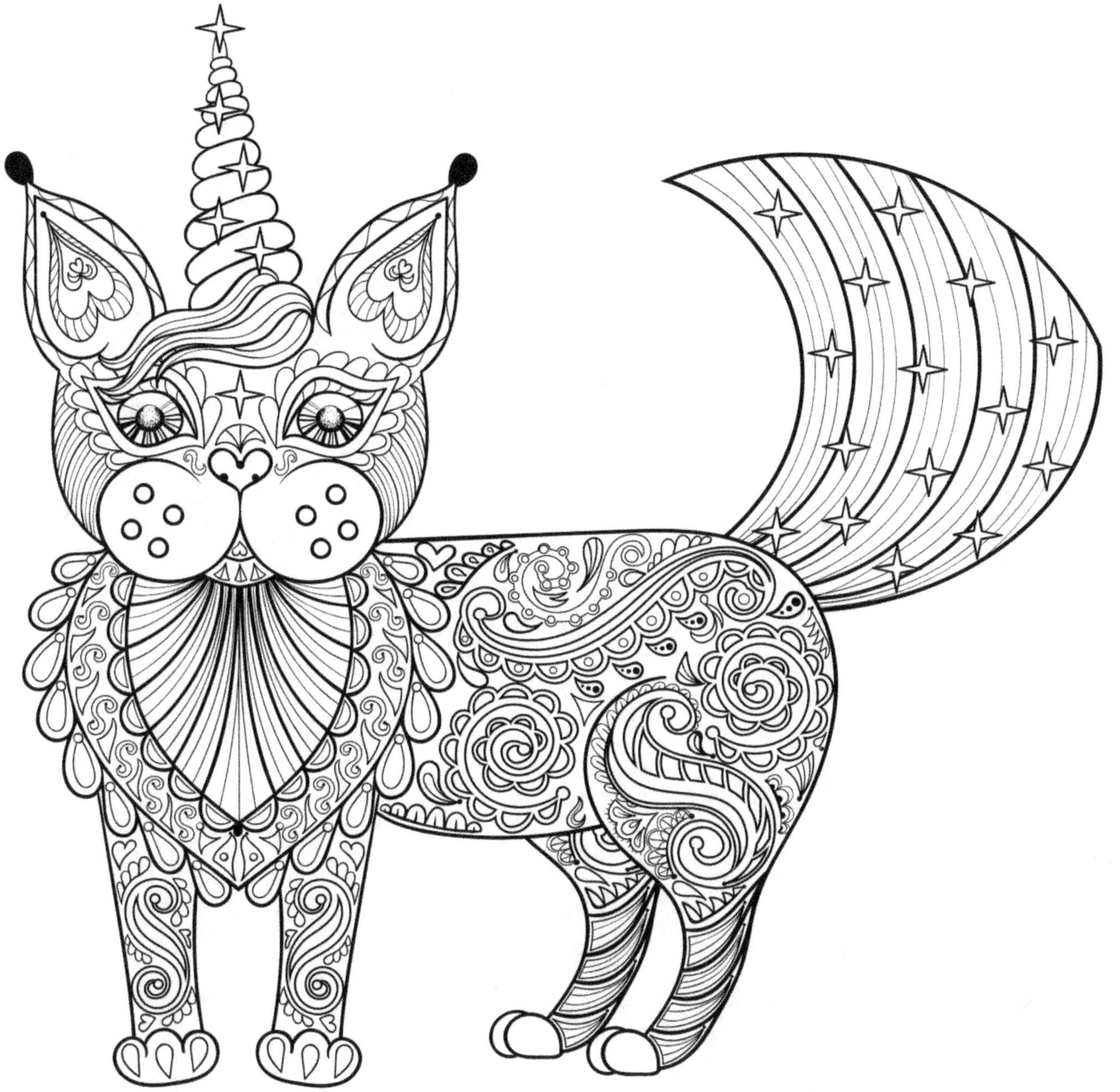

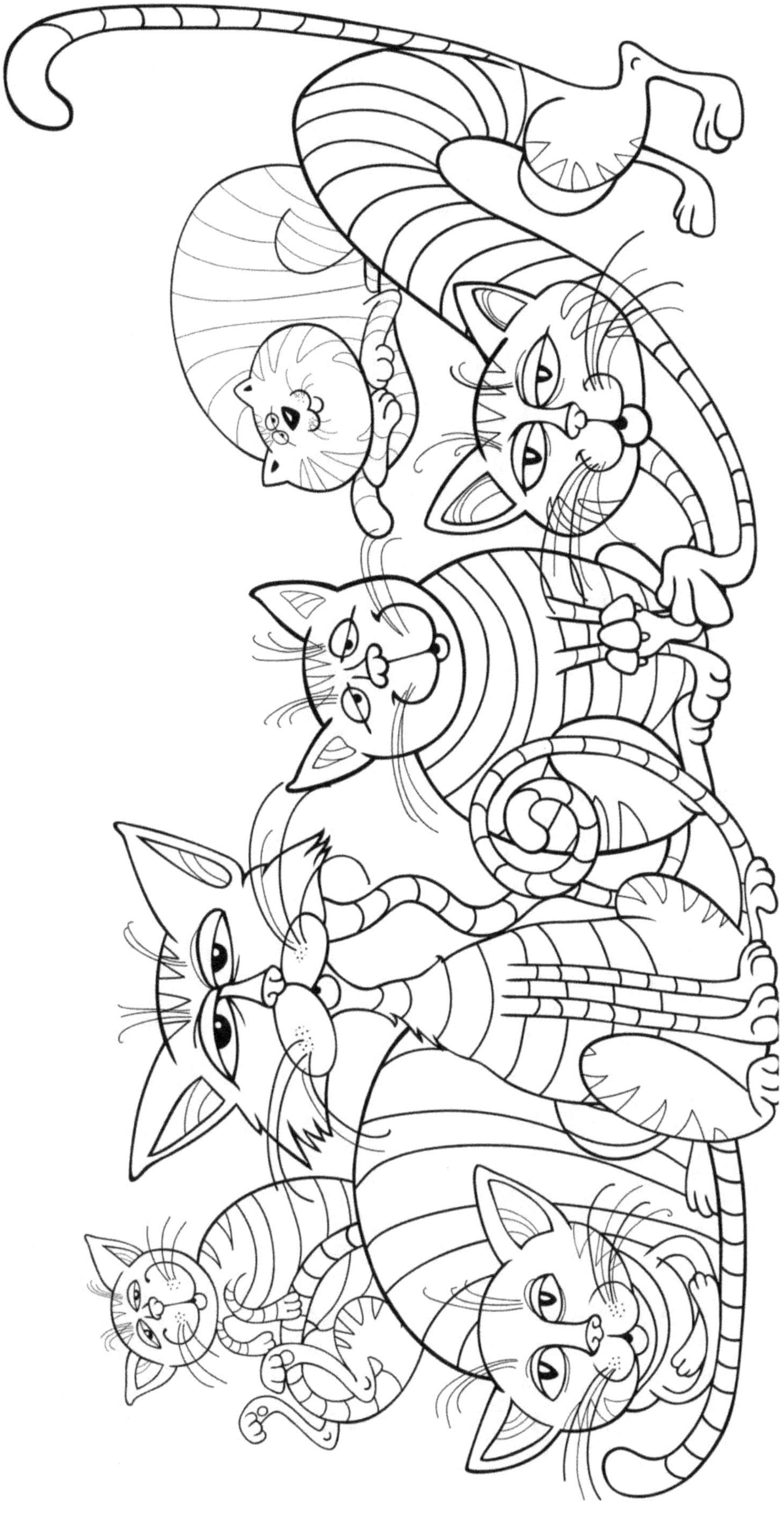

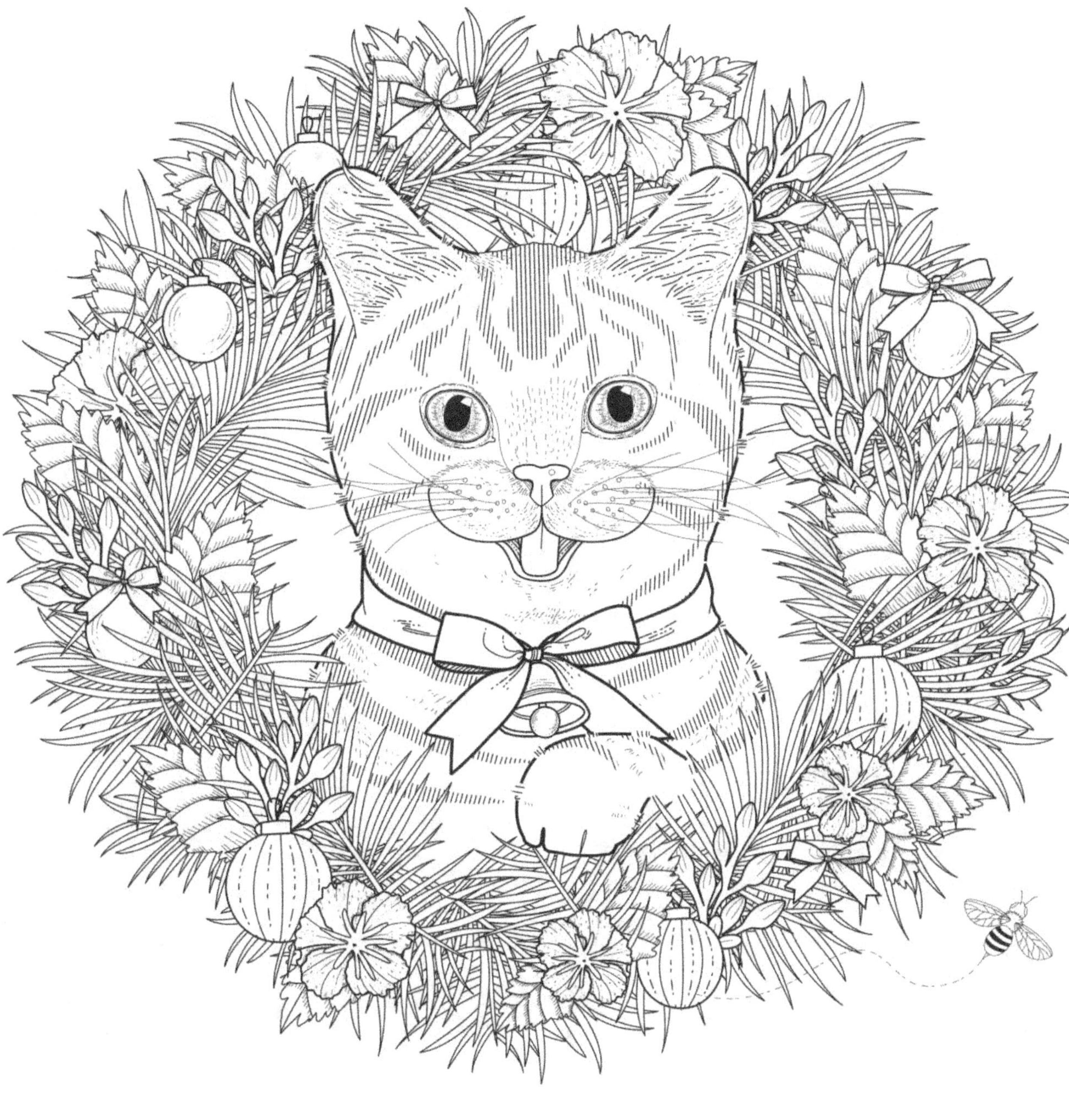

www.ingramcontent.com/pod-product-compliance
Lightning Source LLC
Chambersburg PA
CBHW081856170526
45167CB00007B/3033
9781542992527